THE TECHNIQUES OF JAPANESE EMBROIDERY

THE TECHNIQUES OF JAPANESE EMBROIDERY

Shuji Tamura

The Japanese Embroidery Center

Text and illustrations © Shuji Tamura 1998
The moral right of the author has been asserted.

First published in 1998 by
BT Batsford Ltd
583 Fulham Road
London SW6 5BY

First published in the United States by
Krause Publications

700 E. State St.
Iola, WI 54990-0001
Telephone 715-445-2214

Please call or write for our free catalog of
publications. Our toll-free number to place an order
or obtain a free catalog is 800-258-0929 or please
use our regular business telephone 715-445-2214 for
editorial comment and further information.

Manufactured in Singapore

Designed by DWN Ltd, London

CONTENTS

INTRODUCTION

For more than a thousand years, the working of the embroidery discussed in this book has remained within Japan, growing and developing among professionals through the apprentice system, passing always from master to apprentice orally, acquiring its own unique characteristics. The long isolation of Japan from the rest of the world, so conducive to introspection, was highly favorable to the development of this art form. However, after over a thousand years' sleep, this cultural heritage, the fruit of countless unknown predecessors, is now available to a wider public.

In Japanese, there are many words that end with the character *dō* which describe activities, such as, *sadō, kendō, kyudō, kadō, syodō, judō, kōdō, nui-dō,* and so on. Each word is made up of two parts; the first part represents the physical or technical means of each activity, and the second part, *dō,* stands for the mental and spiritual means employed in 'the way'. For example, the word *sadō* is made up of two parts: *sa* meaning 'tea', and *dō* meaning 'the way'. Usually this is translated as the art of the tea ceremony, but it means much more than making a cup of tea to drink. This ceremony provides an oasis of calm and beauty in the midst of a harsh, everyday existence. The ritual developed to a high art form in order to honor the beauty of the tea ceremony.

Kendō, the art of swordsmanship, first began as a method of self-defense and fighting. Swords have fallen out of favor as a choice of weapons, but the skillful use of the sword is still studied and demonstrated in *kendō* tournaments. As in the tea ceremony, *kendō* tournaments stress politeness and respect for oneself as participant and for one's opponents. The structure helps spectators to see and

Japanese Embroidery Center, Atlanta Georgia.

Classes for children, as well as adults, ensure that Japanese embroidery will be passed on to future generations.

feel the strength within themselves, even though it is the participants who are fighting one another. Using bamboo swords, the opponents try to beat each other, but, throughout the contest, maintaining serenity of mind is always more important than winning or losing.

In the word *nui-dō*, *nui* means embroidery, and *dō* means the way. There are three aspects of *nui-dō*: the acquisition of technical skills and knowledge, the development of sensitivity and awareness, and the constant discovery of the spiritual components of the art of embroidery, resulting in an attitude of peace, calm, and harmony. Great skill alone, that is, only the technical part, does not produce art.

Embroidery came to Japan from China through Korea. After it first arrived in Japan, it was preserved unchanged for many years. But through centuries of evolution, the designs and techniques eventually evolved into their characteristically Japanese forms, and they are now being passed on to you through this book. I only ask that you take sufficient time to make a serious effort to master these special ways of stitching, and that you do not try too soon to adapt them to your own personal style. True mastery requires time and an accurate grasp and appreciation of each basic skill. Only later can these techniques be transposed into your own tradition, there to evolve into a new tradition of lasting value with its own characteristic beauty.

Making our best efforts in both techniques of training and mental discipline, using the traditional techniques described here, can take us beyond the hobby stage. It is my fervent hope that *nui-dō* will play its part in making the world one. When a pebble hits the surface of a pond, the pebble itself sinks to the bottom, but ripples reach out, one after another, across the whole pond. I am hoping this manual will act like a pebble, sending ripple after ripple across the face of every embroidery tradition.

Shuji Tamura

田村 修二

Shuji Tamura 1998

CHAPTER 1

HISTORY OF JAPANESE EMBROIDERY

Wherever the great textile collections of the world are displayed, the phrase 'a lost art' is, all too often, applied to many of the techniques on view. Although Japanese embroidery is more than a thousand years old, it is one of the rare needlework disciplines that has never died out. Since its introduction, it has been worked with a level of technical skill and spiritual devotion rarely encountered in the history of the needle arts. In any piece of embroidery, skillful technique alone does not make good work. Pattern, color, and stitch selection are also very important. These four elements all contribute to the creation of high quality work and have been cultivated in Japan since their introduction.

Traditional Japanese embroidery continues to reflect the lives of the people who stitch the work, as well as the lives of those who use the finished creations. Any attempt to trace the history of this technique will necessarily focus on the *kimono*, the traditional ladies' costume of Japan, and Japanese embroidery's close association with the introduction of Buddhism into early Japan.

1. THE BEGINNING OF EMBROIDERY
(PREHISTORIC PERIOD TO 552 AD)

Most scholars agree that embroidery began as a practical method of repairing or reinforcing garments and household objects. In ancient times, the Japanese took the skins of animals and the bark from trees, sewing them together to the required size for clothing and household items. At this time stitching was utilitarian, a method of joining segments and mending or repairing worn clothing. The Japanese word for embroidery is composed of two elements: *shi*, meaning 'to stick' and *shū* or *nui*, meaning 'to make patterns with thread'. The words *shishū* and *nui* incorporate subtle differences. While *shishū* is used for all types of sewing (including embroidery),

nui represents the embellishment by a professional. Thus *nui-dō* has come to mean 'the way of embroidery'.

From the earliest times down to the present, the Japanese have devised an endless variety of patterns. The patterns had nothing to do with practicality and had no bearing on protecting the body from the cold or the heat. The basis of the Japanese aesthetic sense is the primacy of beauty over practicality or utility. Sewing with a needle thus gradually gave way to the decoration of clothing simply because people wanted to adorn themselves. This has been the case in virtually every country throughout the world. Embroidery has served as the creative outlet for many cultures, producing embellished clothing and household articles which transcend practicality and rationality.

◄◄ An antique *fukusa*, showing temples and shrines in the area of Kyoto. Collection of Jon Eric Riis.

Treasure house (*kura*) at Kurenai-Kai, Japan.

2. EARLY EMBROIDERED BUDDHA FIGURES (ASUKA PERIOD, 552–645)

Although until recent years the primary use of Japanese embroidery has been to decorate clothing, the roots of this silk and metal-thread technique are to be found in religious embroidery. The earliest reference in literature to an embroidered Buddha figure is in a passage in *The Chronicles of Japan*, written in the thirteenth year of the Emperor Suiko (604). Unfortunately, this embroidery did not survive, and we can only guess as to the types of stitches used to execute it.

Buddhism originated in India in about the sixth century BC and was transmitted to China in about the first century AD. It flourished in China during the Northern and Southern Dynasties Period (*c.* 317–589 AD) and was brought to Korea in the second half of the fourth century. In the sixth century, the king of the Paekche dynasty, which ruled northern Korea, sent Buddhist images and *sutra* scrolls to the Yamato court of the Japanese Emperor Kin-mei (539–571), hoping to enlist the Japanese as allies in the war with the Silla dynasty that ruled southern Korea. Many other forms of decorative art were introduced to Japan at this time, including, it is believed, methods for embroidering Buddha figures.

Half a century after Buddhism was introduced to Japan, Shōtoku Taishi, the prince appointed regent by the empress Suiko, became a convert to Buddhism. Prince Shōtoku is one of Japan's foremost cultural heroes. Along with instituting political reforms, he also founded many monasteries, including the Hōryūji, which contains the world's oldest wooden building. He did much to popularize Buddhist worship. After his death, court embroiderers worked an embroidery of Shōtoku Taishi in Paradise with his mother, dedicating their work to his memory. One of these pieces, known as the Tenjukoku Mandala Shūchō, was stitched in 622,

Dormitory at
Kurenai-Kai, Japan

and is the oldest existing example of Japanese embroidery. A reproduction of this embroidery may be seen today at the Chugu-ji convent in Nara, which also owns existing fragments of the original *mandala*.

3. Later Embroidered Buddha Figures (Nara Period, 645–794)

Another representative example of ancient Japanese embroidery is the Shishu Shaka Seppo-zu (Embroidered Depiction of Sakyamuni [Buddha] Preaching) made in the Nara era. It is called the Kajuu-ji Embroidery Album as it was preserved for a long time in Kajuu-ji temple at Yamashina in Kyoto. It has been designated a National Treasure and is presently in the collection of the National Museum at Nara.

The embroidered Buddhas of the Asuka and Nara eras were not made to be objects of reverence as the Buddha figures made of gold, copper and wood were. Rather, the embroideries were made to show in picture form the teachings of Buddha in a way that anyone could understand. They served a similar function to that of stained-glass windows in the Christian cathedrals of Europe. They added an atmosphere of solemnity to the halls of Buddhist temples, while also conveying some point of religious teaching. The primary stitches used to create these early works were *sagara-nui* (knots), *kusari-nui* (chain-stitch), *tsugibari-nui* (double running stitch), and *kaeshi-nui* (outline stitch). They were stitched using a twisted silk thread, and both the design areas and the background were usually solidly filled, showing little or none of the fabric ground. Although these stitches did not require a high level of technical skill, the true artistry of the embroiderers may be found in the accurate depiction of the smallest details, particularly the facial expressions and musculature of the Buddha figure.

In the Heian era, which followed, embroidered Buddhas gradually gave way to painted depictions, though very little work has survived from this period. The embroidered Buddha figure did not emerge again until the Kamakura era, a time in which the Pure Land sect of Buddhism replaced the Shingon and Tendai sects. The result was the spread of Buddhism beyond the nobility to the masses. Buddhism in this era changed greatly in form and in content, teaching that, no matter what their station in life, those who performed good works and chanted 'Amida Buddha', could go to the Pure Land paradise after death. By the Kamakura and Muromachi eras, the embroidery of Buddha figures was done more for individual veneration during morning and evening prayers than for the decoration of temples. For this reason, the stitches used changed from bold, unrefined ones, to *sashi-nui* (Realistic technique). Satin stitches and thin linear effects using a single thread imparted feelings of softness and warmth. The embroidered Buddhas were intended for personal use in small home altars, rather than for public exhibition in temples. Perhaps it is because they were not objects of public scrutiny or approval that there was very little discipline, and the quality of execution of the work declined.

4. Development of Native Style (Heian Period, 794–1185)

Although Japan has been willingly influenced by foreign cultures at certain points in its history, it has largely remained isolated from the world beyond its shores. Ideas adopted from other places were transformed, evolving into something uniquely Japanese. Clothing with distinctively Japanese characteristics came to be worn in the latter half of the tenth century. Society drew on the Confucian vision of a network of hierarchical relationships, and the rank of Heian court members could be divined from both the color and decoration of their costumes.

For ladies of the aristocratic class, clothing served not only to protect the wearer from the cold, but also to indicate personal status, and it became the custom to wear multiple layers of clothing. In selecting these, each of a different shade of color, court ladies created beautiful rhythms of color with layered collars, sleeves, and hems. These different layers of color were known as *kasane no irome,*

Exhibition of *obi* at Kurenai-Kai, Japan.

'layered color tones' (*irome* also suggests 'alluring' or 'seductive'). Some of the color sequences resulting from these combinations were named after flowers. The appreciation shown by the Heian nobles for flowering plants, and the seasonal changes in them, was reflected in the sensitivity of their color choices and the ingenuity with which they dyed their fabrics.

While the combination of colors used was primarily based on the practice of layering, these combinations gradually changed over the years. Personal preferences also came to play a role. Color schemes based on layering and tones based on the seasons have survived even in modern clothing and are a part of present-day customs. The color combinations for the *haori* (short coat) and *han-eri* (half-collar) for the *kimono*, the *obi-jime* (cord for the *obi*) and the *obi* (sash), and for the front part and lining of the *kimono* are evidence of the outstanding color sensibilities of the Japanese people. It was not until the Muromachi era (1392–1568) and later that the *kimono* was decorated in the form of the *kosode*, worn as an outer garment, with a variety of colors woven into it.

5. YŪSHOKU PATTERN DEVELOPMENT (KAMAKURA PERIOD, 1185–1392)

In producing a work of embroidery, the most important element was the design. Foreign culture had had a great influence on Japan in the Asuka and Nara eras and it was during these periods that the truly international culture of the Chinese T'ang Dynasty (618–*c.* 907) was deeply assimilated in Japan. Official contact with the T'ang was broken off at the beginning of the Heian era, however. In time, the influences received from the T'ang underwent a period of adjustment, and for the next four hundred years the refinement of the imperial court was the focus of cultural life in Japan, an influence which continues to the present day.

Chinese characters were introduced to Japan along with Buddhism around the fifth or sixth century AD. Approximately four or five hundred years after that, the uniquely Japanese *kana* syllabary system of writing was developed. In addition, Chinese clothing was worn in the Asuka and Nara eras, as seen in the courtly dress at the time of Shōtoku Taishi. Clothing with distinctively Japanese characteristics came to be worn in the latter half of the tenth century. This consisted of full court dress for males and *jūni-hitoe* (twelve-layered dress) worn by females. The color of these dresses was determined by rank. For males of the fourth rank and above, the colour was black, for the fifth rank it was scarlet, and for those of the sixth rank and below it was blue. The patterns used were also determined by rank.

In that era, practicing the rites of the imperial court was known as *yūshiki* (literally, 'having knowledge'), and those taking part were known as *yūshikisha*. In the beginning, those who followed the practices and usages of the Heian court and military (which included embroidery patterns) regulated and recorded the correct form for rites, ceremonies and clothing for the imperial court, in accordance with the ancient rules. They breathed life into these practices and attained a height of courtly elegance which was passed on to future generations.

By the middle of the Heian era, the court nobles made a great pretense of their family lineage, held steadfast to their family names, and gave themselves empty formalities. Eventually these court nobles yielded political power to the newly emerged warrior class. With this, decorative patterns were gradually transformed. In the Kamakura era, specific patterns came to be used which made distinctions on the basis of rank and family standing. These were known as *yūsoku* patterns – they bespoke the standing of people well versed in ancient court and military practices – and they were to set the tone for Japanese embroidery patterns thereafter.

Thus it was that there was a transition from *yūshiki* ('people with knowledge') patterns to *yūsoku* ('people with professional rank') patterns. In the embroidery circles of today's Japan, the word *yūshoku* (which is the same as *yūsoku*) is used to denote patterns which are created by arranging a motif from the natural world, modified or simplified to emphasize its most prominent characteristics.

6. Nō DANCE COSTUME
(MUROMACHI PERIOD, 1392–1568)

Initially *Nō* was performed by players wearing their everyday clothing. So moved were the noble audiences of that era by the acting that they supposedly used to remove some of their clothing and give it to the actors. This was called *kazuke-mono* ('reward clothing'). It was also the custom for the actor who was the recipient of this clothing to put it on and at once perform a dance. The actors were thus able to bring an extra dimension to the drama by using the costly garments they had received from the influential people of the day as costumes for the stage.

Costume for the classical *Nō* drama was also a strong influence on clothing in general. Everything in this form of drama depended on the art of the performers, and both the acting and the costumes became separated from reality and transformed into symbols that led the audience into the realm of illusion. Actors in the *Nō* began to wear robes called *kari-ginu*, made of fabrics called *suikan* or *karaori*, heavy Chinese brocade or Japanese fabric woven in imitation of it. The *kari-ginu* was a garment for hunting, with long, wide sleeves which had drawstrings at the wrists for convenience during the chase. The actors were thus able to take off their physical selves and use the linear contours of the costumes to exude an atmosphere of the fantastic. It was not until the Momoyama Period and later that costumes made expressly for the *Nō* drama came to be worn.

Costumes for young female roles were known as *iro-iri* ('including red') and were a colorful shade of red. Costumes for older female roles contained no red and were known as *iro-nashi* ('without red'). The color white was used to symbolize a sacred or holy character. There are many examples of *karaori* costumes in which designs depicting flowering plants were used to show femininity. Designs using lions, clouds, and thunder were used on *atsu-ita* (heavy robes) to portray male strength. Beautiful patterns of embroidery and *suri-haku* ('rubbed metal leaf') are used in the *Nō* costume known as *nui-haku* ('the combination of embroidery and metal leaf'). Suited to female roles, *suri-haku* is worn by winding the cloth around the waist and letting the sleeves droop down behind to form a *koshimaki*. *Karaori* and other such garments were worn over this so that only the hem was visible, even though a beautiful pattern was stitched all over the undergarment. *Nui-haku* (embroidery with metal leaf) was used not only for female roles but also for roles depicting the emperor, court nobles and infant prodigies, and for other roles which required an air of nobility and gentility.

The *Nō* drama had replaced *gagaku*, the ceremonial music of the court nobles passed down from ancient times. It came under the patronage of the rulers as the official drama and had developed accordingly. In the Edo Period the wealth and power of the *shōgun* and *daimyo* (feudal lords) and improvements in embroidering and dyeing techniques provided a backdrop to *Nō* costumes – in shape, color, pattern and materials – and helped perfect the unique art seen in *Nō* drama today.

7. DEVELOPMENT OF THE KOSODE (MOMOYAMA PERIOD, 1568–1615)

Since the Heian era, central political power had been gradually transferred from the court nobles to the warrior class. The history of the Muromachi era in Japan had been one of prolonged upheavals, combined with cultural achievement. The majority of the feudal *daimyo* in the Momoyama era were warriors who had once belonged to the lower classes. This led to a situation called *gekokujō*, a time when 'those beneath supersede those on top'. The fact that *shōgun* Toyotomi Hideyoshi, who had been born into poverty, became ruler is without parallel in Japanese history. We can see this same background of the ruled dominating the rulers even in the development of clothing.

The *kosode* ('small-sleeved garment'), which is the basis for all modern *kimono*, is a product of the Heian era. In that era, the court nobles wore *ōsode* ('large-sleeved garment') as an outer garment,

Workshop of Kurenai
- Kai, Japan

whereas the *kosode* was worn right inside the *ōsode*, which made it function very much like an undergarment. The *kosode* was used among the lower classes and the common people as work clothing and everyday clothing. Once the ruled came to dominate the rulers, the dress and ornamentation of the upper classes became simpler and more informal, while the lower classes, whose social station had improved, demanded that the quality of the popular *kosode* be improved as well. Gradually the *kosode* came to be worn by all segments of Japanese society.

Even though the colors and the patterns of the individual *jūni-hitoe* ('twelve-layered dress') of the Heian era were simple, a sophisticated beauty could be expressed by layering the clothes at the collar, sleeve and hem. When the shape of the garment became standardized to a single long piece of clothing, the *kosode*, great pains were taken with various techniques, designs, and colors to decorate this simple outside garment.

In the Momoyama era, the break with tradition was expressed by a new artistic spirit brimming with originality. Designs of multicolored splendor met the needs of the age. Patterns could not be expressed as freely in weaving as in embroidery which thus came into increasing use. A great number of these works of art have been handed down to the present day.

One can use these works to study the characteristics of the embroidery of that age. Stitches used included *nuki-jibiki* (weft foundation layer), *nari-jibiki* (horizontal foundation layer) and *nuikiri* (diagonal single layer). The main techniques generally used flat silk thread. *Matsui-nui* (line of staggered diagonals) and *hippari-toji* (line of held thread), both involving holding the foundation thread down, were used to show the demarcation between flower petals, to indicate veins in leaves, or to delineate borders of designs. The use of thick flat silk and long stitches created a rich, bold feeling.

By making distinct use of right and left slanting stitches for the diagonal *nuikiri*, the embroiderer was able to depict motion and add expression and greater realism to the pattern. Warm colors were used frequently, especially gold, and

could be said to symbolize this era. A brand-new embroidery technique used at this time involved abrupt shifts of color in the same pattern and is said to have been influenced by an embroidery technique which was brought back from a trade expedition to Ming Dynasty China.

8. KEICHO KOSODE (EARLY EDO PERIOD, C. 1596–1615)

The very earliest years of the Edo Period are known as the Keicho Period. By this time, after scarcely less than half a century, the *kosode* of the Momoyama period had been transformed into its exact opposite. What, then, had brought about this great change? A look at the social background of that era may throw light on this question, which has become something of a mystery. The Muromachi and Momoyama eras saw the old social order overturned, and most of the new ruling class had formerly been of inferior status. According to an edict of 1591, social status and occupation were to be strictly controlled through a rigid class system for the military, agricultural, craft, and merchant classes, in that order. In 1615 the *shōgunate* promulgated ordinances to regulate the *daimyo*, and others to control the conduct of the court and the court nobles. The *shōgunate* also passed religious decrees to bring Buddhist temples and monasteries under its control. In 1616 restrictions were placed on trade, and in 1639 the entire country was sealed off.

As this dark feudal era was ushered in, there was a break with the vivid colors characteristic of the Momoyama era. The feelings and lives of the people were now deeply connected to the feudalism of the day, and the *kosode* of the Keicho era soon became distinct from the *kosode* of the Momoyama. In the Momoyama period, the color tones were generally bright and the patterns concrete, with *suri-haku* (rubbed metal leaf), and embroidery mainly used for vertical figures. Embroidery was worked with thick thread and long stitches. It was relaxed, large scale, not delicate. In the Keicho *kosode* the color tones were generally dark, with deep red predominating, and purple, brown, and black following close behind. The red was inspired by the blood of those executed in the early days of the regime, as a result of the persecution of Christians and political purges. The abstract patterns, tiny and detailed, were not readily understood. Embroidery, tie-dye, and gold leaf were all used, often in combination.

These differences suggest a people searching for beauty in a world with severe constraints. The natural desire looks smudged that wells up in the soul gave birth to the unique beauty of the Keicho *kosode*, which captivated the hearts of the Japanese people even in the midst of gloom and sorrow. By looking at the garments of that period, we can understand how the Japanese were animated by that unique beauty which springs from creative energy and how, undaunted by privation, they did not give in to the repression of the times. In Edo (now called Tokyo) in 1657 and in Kyoto in 1661, fires which destroyed vast quantities of the possessions of the wealthy had a strong influence on the designs of the period. Tie-dye was emphasized, since large areas could be embellished with less effort than embroidery, which was now reserved for smaller areas. The use of negative space also entered into the composition.

9. DEVELOPMENT OF THE OBI (MID-EDO PERIOD, –1868)

The word *obi* comes from the Japanese word *obu/musubu*, which means 'to put on the body'. The practice of wearing an *obi* over an outer garment can be seen in the ancient *haniwa* (baked clay figures), made when people believed that *obi* had magical powers. The *obi* that we see today, however, was originally used to tie a garment. In order not to detract from the beauty of the *kosode*, the *obi* of the Muromachi and Momoyama eras were simple and abbreviated. Measuring approximately 3 yd in length and 3 in to nearly 3⅜ in in width, they were used to cinch the front of the garment.

In the Keicho Period (early Edo era), however, the *obi* became wider, increasing from 4⅜–5⅞ in to 7½–9 in, and eventually becoming nearly 15 in wide and 5 yd long. At the same time, the manner of

tying the *obi* became flashier, and a fashion statement. The *taiko-musubi* ('bridge on the river'), which is the style most generally used today, came into fashion. It imitated the type of *obi* worn by geisha associated with the *taiko-bashi* ('drum bridge') of the Kameido Shrine in Tokyo.

Gradually the *obi* became wider still, and the decorative elements became stronger. These changes meant that the *obi* now functioned as a long piece of cloth that bisected the body. The pattern and composition of the *kosode* changed greatly. By the beginning of the Edo era, a single *kosode* had become just one display area with large designs. As the *obi* developed, the patterns of the *kosode* developed also. Among them were *chirashi* (scattered) patterns that were quite natural, even though they were interrupted by the *obi*, geometrical patterns composed of stripes, grids or lattices, and patterns which ran up and down the garment and incorporated the *obi*. Finally, patterns for the hem and the shoulders of the *kosode* developed.

Now that women had been freed of the thick layered robes of the Heian era and were girding themselves with a wide *obi*, which accentuated the beauty of feminine dress, the *kosode* again became a formal garment, and the function of the *obi* reverted to that of a tie. This was a bold fashion statement, expressed in the *taiko-musubi* style of the *obi* by ingenious dyeing and embroidery techniques. The development of the wide *obi* meant great changes for embroidery. For the *kimono*, which was made of thin material, most embroidered patterns were light. Thicker materials were used for the *obi*, and appropriate stitching was chosen for this. Several types of embroidery techniques were used in sequence – first, a foundation layer of stitching, then padding, superimposed figures, short-stitch holding, and, finally, outlining of the figures with couched threads. This heavy style of embroidery, with one technique superimposed on another, was seen as an expression of the utmost dignity, and is regarded as most typical of Japanese work.

One of the many policies promulgated to stabilize the Tokugawa *shōgunate* was a status system which determined one's station at birth and put

A Japanese lady in formal costume, wearing a *taiko-musubi* style.

restrictions on the most obvious symbol of that status, clothing. Included were sumptuary laws issued by the fifth *shōgun* Tsunayoshi in 1683 under which expensive *kimono* cloth and embroidery were prohibited: 'No *kosode* exceeding 100 monme in value (presently yen 100,000) can be made. Those who own them may not wear them'. Such harsh restrictions were the order of the day and the *kosode* came to be an object of prohibition rather than a subject of beauty or utility. Many methods were found to circumvent these prohibitions. Elaborate linings were sewn inside simple garments.

10. THE DEVELOPMENT OF THE HAN-ERI (MEIJI PERIOD, 1868–1912, AND TAISHO PERIOD, 1912–1926)

At this time a new opportunity for embroidery presented itself, the *han-eri*, or half-collar. In Japanese etiquette it was considered too direct to look another person straight in the eye, so, when people first meet, their eyes go to the collar, which is near the throat, considered an important part of the person. One shows respect for another by straightening one's collar. The custom of making a display of a beautiful collar goes back to the 'layered color tones' of the Heian era, when people sought to contrast colors at the collar of the *kosode* as well as at the sleeve and at the hem. The aesthetic sensibility which linked these layers of color to seasonal flowers and other natural phenomena is used in clothing even today. A general sensitivity to color is prized by the Japanese and evident in the ideal of the *kimono*, which changes with the seasons. It is evident as well in the *haori* and the *obi*, which are chosen to match the *kimono* just as the color and pattern of the *han-eri* are chosen.

The *han-eri* (half-collar) is so called because it is half as long as a full collar and half as wide as a full fabric. Collars were easily soiled, so the *han-eri* was a practical solution – although not washable, it could be used and then discarded. It was in the later half of the Edo era that the collar came to be decorated with beautiful patterns. From the Meiji through the Taisho eras *yuzen-eri* (printed collars), *shibori-eri* (tie-dyed collars), *nui-eri* (embroidered collars) and *eri* of other expensive materials were made. The Japanese saying, 'You can tell what is in style by looking at the *eri*', is witness to this fashion. The ingenious designs and techniques which have survived to the present are an indication of the splendor of that age.

The collar was shaped to cross the neck at a bold incline to contrast with the oval of the face and to lend it shape and balance. The *han-eri* was meant to be used in everyday life, and, as a result, embroidery techniques used for it were unique. *Kawari-nui* ('novel effects') stitching, based on fundamental techniques which placed special emphasis on the way the stitches lined up to the weft direction, was often used. From this there sprang a variety of embroidery techniques which were a product of the embroiderer's passing fancy – whatever seemed interesting or caught the eye. These *kawari-nui* (techniques unique to the *han-eri*) were thought up in great numbers to set off the face and frame it in ever-changing ways. These novel effects were, however, not meant to be used with *kimono* and *obi*, which tried to present an air of grace and dignity.

11. DISPERSION TO THE JAPANESE PUBLIC (SHŌWA PERIOD, 1926–1989)

After World War II, people in Japan were somewhat indifferent to Japanese embroidery which was, after all, a sophisticated technique. In its stead, foreign embroidery (especially that from Europe) caught on and was accepted by a great number of people. Today foreign embroidery techniques are accepted and used by many in Japan, and quilting, too, is enjoying great popularity. Japanese embroidery, then, is a traditional art form which has been passed down through the master/apprentice system for over a thousand years. Even though it has been in and out of favor depending on the whims and caprices of the social order, it has been transmitted to us by that same social order without interruption. While the finest work was, for most of its history, the product of professionals, some simple embroidery was taught in the public schools until recent years. Now,

◀◀ An ox cart (*gosho-guruma*) of the type used by the imperial family.

Han-eri (half-collars).

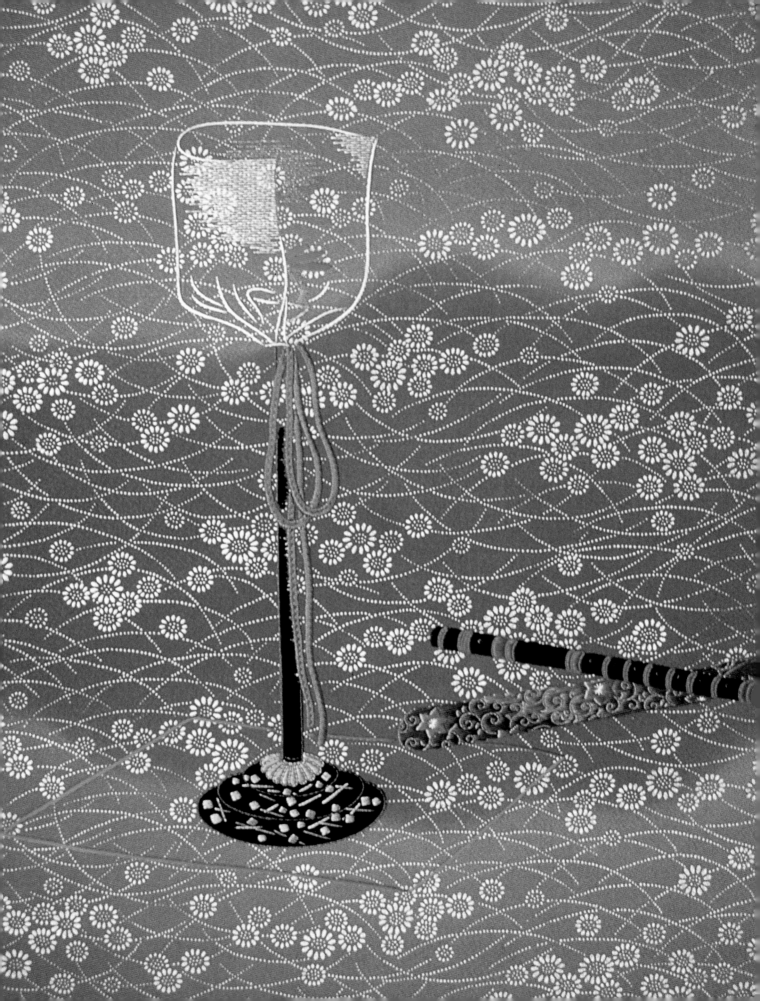

however, with the decline in the popularity of the *kimono*, it survives only through schools which offer a degree in fashion design or through a handful of teachers.

Into this tradition came the late Master Iwao Saito, founding the Kurenai-Kai Community in Togane City in 1965. Saito recognized Japanese embroidery as a tradition when he was about fifty-five years old. Until then he saw it as a job, but not as a mission. Only then did he recognize the sixteen hundred years of tradition and his obligation to pass it on. In addition to teaching apprentices at Kurenai-Kai, he established classes in many cities.

In 1970, Saito, who learned from his master as an apprentice in the traditional oral way, decided to open the door to the general public by writing down the techniques, planning a curriculum, publishing a textbook and teaching these techniques to students of embroidery in Japan. In 1972, young Shuji Tamura joined the community. Side by side, they taught all over Japan: Sendai, Tokyo, Nagoya, Osaka, Hiroshima, Fukuoka, and Kagoshima. While teaching, Saito was still producing new works. In 1976 Kurenai-Kai began holding its own exhibitions, which continue today. Over time Saito also published numerous books and portfolios of designs. The community continues to publish a small journal.

Saito's only son, Shinsaku, had already joined him in his life's work in 1965. Today he is president of the community in Japan. Saito's daughter, Masa, studied Japanese painting at university and joined the workshop after graduation. In order to assure the continuance of the tradition, Saito selected as his successor his son-in-law Shuji Tamura, through whom he believed that the tradition would be even better transmitted than through himself. In 1980 Tamura brought works from Kurenai-Kai to the national seminar of the Embroiderers' Guild of America, held that year in Dallas, Texas. The following year Mr. and Mrs. Tamura began teaching the first formal classes outside Japan.

12. WORLD-WIDE EXPANSION (HEISEI PERIOD, 1989–)

In 1989 the Japanese Embroidery Center was established in Dunwoody, Georgia, USA, opening a door to Japanese embroidery for the English-speaking world. In 1991, classes began in England, and, since then, classes have been running in Australia, Canada, and New Zealand. Many graduates of the ten-phase core curriculum, some from each of these countries, have joined the corps of teachers.

In the future there will be new ways of both creating and teaching. Since the sixteenth century, Japanese embroidery has been used primarily for ladies' clothing. The shape of the *kimono*, the typical costume, changed very little over the centuries, though decorative styles changed, and the creative knowledge has been passed down through the master/apprentice system. As the twentieth century draws to a close, however, Japanese embroidery has taken a bold new step into the world of interior design. With the diminished use of the *kimono*, the increased influence of western style in Japanese homes, and the spread of knowledge of Japanese embroidery throughout the world, the trend is towards embroidery for the home. Each year Japanese students come to the United States to study and to see how embroidery is used to decorate western interiors. Thus the fruits of the labors of myriad anonymous embroiderers of the past can help to bring a desire for unity in the world, based on the concept of nui-dō.

◀◀ An antique lamp and flute symbolize an evening devoted to music, while the gold leaf chrysanthemum pattern in the background indicates the autumn season.

CHAPTER 2

THE MOTIFS OF JAPANESE EMBROIDERY

Among the many unique aspects of Japanese embroidery is its use of motifs which have a symbolic connotation. These symbolic elements have been in use for so long and by such a broad spectrum of people that they are used almost as a form of shorthand. Japanese people from all walks of life and every social station understand their meaning and use them to convey the same message. This practice was nurtured by periodic isolation, when Japan was virtually closed to the outside world and looked inward on itself. It would be far more difficult to create contemporary embroideries without this wealth of tradition and cultural heritage from which to draw. As it is, anyone can draw on the accumulated knowledge, wisdom and experience of countless anonymous predecessors and embroiderers.

Motifs come from a tremendous variety of sources, simple and complex, peasant and noble, illiterate and erudite. They reveal the significant early influence of China, and, later, Europe on Japan, and demonstrate an active awareness of history. They are evidence of the close relationship between nature and daily life in Japanese culture.

The first contacts between China and Japan came perhaps as early as the sixth century AD. Japan adopted the system of Chinese characters in the eighth century, one of an incalculable number of

◀◀ Antique *fukusa* illustrating a Japanese story. Collection of Jon Eric Riis.

Fig. 1

valuable things borrowed from China. In the Asuka Period (552–645) in the eighth century, Buddhism appeared in Japan, bringing with it design motifs that may have traveled the length of the Silk Road. During the Nara Period (645–794), China's influence increased dramatically with the sending of Japanese ambassadors to China specifically to learn about Chinese culture. Among the embroidery motifs which have their origin in Chinese mythology are the phoenix and the paulownia tree (Fig. 2). The phoenix is the mythological bird of China which, according to legend, feeds only from the berries of the paulownia. The animals of the zodiac are also borrowed from Chinese mythology (Fig. 1).

In the following Heian Period (794–1185) the sending of ambassadors was discontinued, and the Japanese tradition of symbolism turned inward on itself and began its independent development. Although there were times when the use of embroidery was restricted, either by cost or by sumptuary laws, it did not necessarily follow that only simple, mundane motifs would be used.

Birds and animals are often found in Japanese embroidery. The most popular bird is the crane (Fig. 3), which represents a wish for longevity. The crane (as with any bird) carries seeds within its body, and is thus considered to bring new life. Mandarin ducks, which mate for life, represent marital fidelity. Swallows are the birds which, in mythology, taught the progenitors of the Japanese people, the god and goddess Izanagi and Izanami, how to make love. Each year on the annual festival of Tanabata, swallows form a bridge over which the star couple of the Weaver and the Cowherd (Altair and Vega) can pass to be together.

The tortoise shares with the crane the quality of longevity, possibly because its life span is so lengthy that long, streaming moss sometimes grows from its shell. Awkward and slow, it lacks the grace of the crane, and so it is generally depicted in stylized form by the hexagon, either as an overall pattern (*kikkō*, Fig. 4) or in lone or grouped motifs. Another marine animal, the shrimp (Fig. 5), is a common motif used in New Year decorations. This pattern represents the bounty of the sea and provides a red

Fig. 2

Fig. 3

Fig. 4

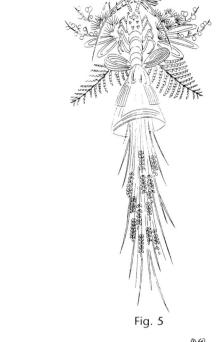

Fig. 5

Fig. 6

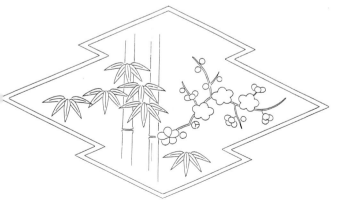

Fig. 7

color, which is rare in winter motifs. With its long tail and hard shell it moves slowly but can also dart quickly. The shell, when dried, is considered to have medicinal properties (especially useful for treating measles), so it is hung under the eaves of the house, to be available when needed. Even insects are represented in embroidery. Grasshoppers and dragonflies appear amid the autumn grasses.

From the countless plants which grow in autumn, seven have been selected since the Nara Period to represent that season symbolically: bush clover, pampas grass, arrowroot, pinks, valerian, eupatorium, and bell flower (Fig. 6). When used as an embroidery motif, these plants provide the three primary colors. However, the seven wild herbs of spring traditionally associated with the end of winter (water parsley, shepherd's purse, cudweed, chickweed, hen-bit, white turnip, and white radish) were originally linked with that season for a more practical reason, because they provided vitamins missing in the meager late-winter diet.

Plum, pine, and bamboo ('the three friends of winter') appear together as auspicious symbols, often under their Chinese name of *shō-chiku-bai* (Fig. 7). They are often used as decorations for New Year and also have individual meanings. The pine and the bamboo symbolize endurance, since they remain green throughout the winter. The unchanging appearance of the pine, despite the passing of the seasons, brings a feeling of good luck and happiness. Because of its long life it is also considered a symbol of longevity. In embroidery, it is sometimes shown by the needles only, by new shoots and needles, or by open cones, as well as by the entire tree. Since bamboo grows quickly to its full height, it is considered to be full of strength, indicating nobility, purity, honesty, and serious character. The plum, which blooms while there is still snow on the branches, symbolizes new hope and, since an old, bent tree still produces a profusion of blossoms, it also stands for longevity.

Ferns, by the multiplicity of their spores, suggest a wish for prosperity, and fans, because of their broadening size, a wish for increase. Parental hopes are expressed by the flax-leaf pattern (Fig. 8),

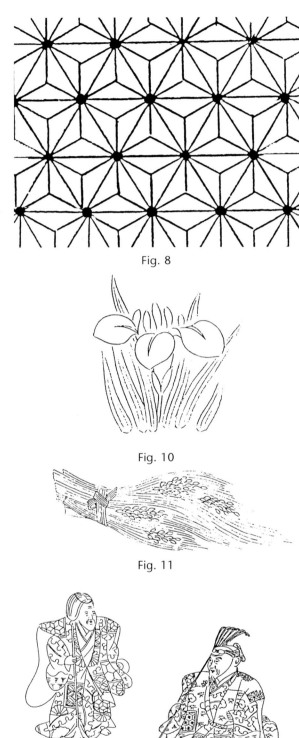

Fig. 8

Fig. 9

Fig. 10

Fig. 11

▶▶ Antique *fukusa* featuring a flower ball (*kusudama*) and fan, while a bamboo curtain can be seen from behind the clouds. Collection of Jon Eric Riis.

Fig. 12

which reflects the wish that children will grow straight and strong.

Nature provides many symbols. The wave pattern, *seikaiha* (Fig. 9), spoke to the *samurai* of the alternation of offense and defense in war. To the general populace it signified a bountiful harvest of both fish and edible sea plants. Overlapping diamonds stand for pine bark. As the seasons pass, each one is evoked by certain plants. Beloved of the Japanese is the cherry tree. Paradoxically, as its petals fall without withering, it is one of the symbols of the *samurai* who had to be ready to give his life instantly. The month of May brings the flowers of the Japanese water iris (Fig. 10), which, in embroidery, is always accompanied by water, even if it is implied rather than shown. Wisteria is typical of June, followed closely by the hydrangea. Late summer's flower is the morning glory. Rice (Fig. 11), of course, is the most important harvest of autumn, and in winter the cedar bows beneath the weight of the snow. At the end of the year, the narcissus, waiting for spring, brings the year full circle.

Folklore provides a plentiful source of motifs. The legend of *Jō* and *Uba* the 'Old Couple of Takasago' (Fig. 12), tells of an old man and woman who were given the care of the pine forest. Every night she would sweep out the old needles, representing bad luck, and he would rake in the good luck. Even when the couple are not shown, the

rake and the broom convey the essence of this story and carry a wish for marital happiness.

The magic sedge hat (Fig. 13), magic straw rain cape (Fig. 14), wooden mallet (Fig. 15), ball (Fig. 16, sometimes pictured with a flame), balance-scale weight (Fig. 17), storehouse key (Fig. 18), and the bottomless purse (Fig. 19) are commonly considered the seven traditional treasures, *takarazukushi*. Although these are the most usual selection, there are many other motifs which are occasionally used. Both the cape and hat render the

wearer invisible. Swinging the magic mallet will make dreams come true. Wishes will be granted when you rub the magic ball. As for the balance-scale weight, a *samurai* on his way to battle would have his gold cast in this shape – because it is symmetrical, no part could be taken without detection, and therefore his wealth was protected. Since protection from fire and theft was especially important, valuables were placed in a masonry storehouse called a *kura*, the key of which is associated with ancient times. Motifs of military

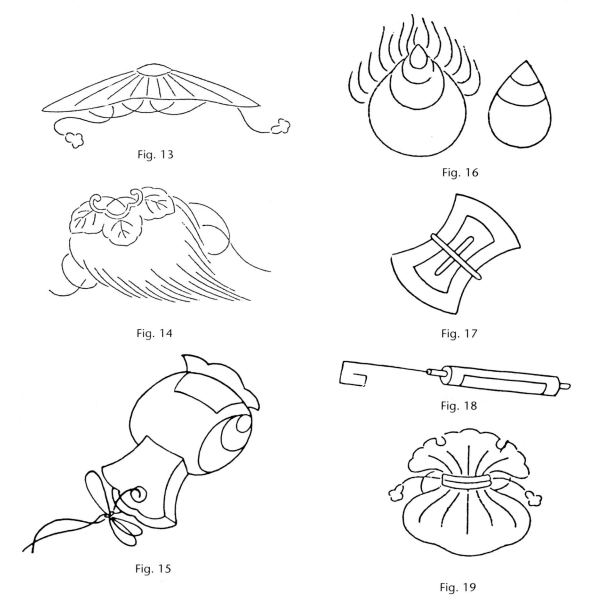

Fig. 13

Fig. 16

Fig. 14

Fig. 17

Fig. 18

Fig. 15

Fig. 19

equipment might signify parents' wishes for their son to have the strength and heart of a true warrior.

Some shapes are not so easy to comprehend. Rhinoceros horn (Fig. 20) was used as a medicine for fever. Silk was once entirely imported, rare, and valuable, therefore silk rolls (Fig. 21) denote a wish for wealth. The cross (Fig. 22) is a symbol of expansiveness. Also included in some treasure designs is the clove (Fig. 23), valued for its rarity and its many uses: scent, flavoring, dyestuff, medicine,

and even insect repellent! Scrolls tell us of the value placed on knowledge. Often all of these treasures are depicted on a treasure ship (Fig. 24). An island nation, Japan depended on the outside world for inspiration, innovation, and expensive consumer goods. In the abstract, the ship came to symbolize all of the good things that could arrive by ship, from abroad or from other parts of the country.

The pattern of overlapping circles called *shippō* (Fig. 25) was probably originally named *shi* (four) *ho*

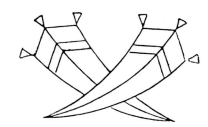

Fig. 20

Fig. 23

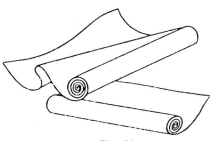

Fig. 21

Fig. 24

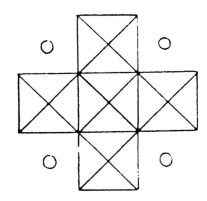

Fig. 22

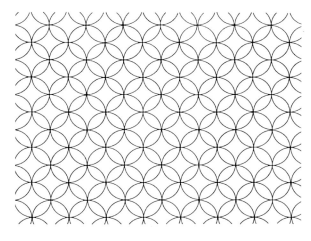

Fig. 25

(directions), and the word evolved into *shippō*. The pattern symbolizes expansiveness.

The five traditional and universal festivals of the Japanese year are the New Year (the first day of the first month), the Doll Festival (also called the Peach Festival or Girls' Day, the third day of the third month), Boys' Day (now celebrated as Children's Day, the fifth day of the fifth month), Tanabata, with its double association of stars and handwork such as weaving (the seventh day of the seventh month), and the Chrysanthemum Festival on the ninth day of the ninth month. Each festival has its own symbols to represent it. Among those for New Year are *noshi* and *shō-chiku-bai*. Noshi (Fig. 26) were originally strips of dried and stretched abalone. These, along with *sake*, were given with every gift, to signify the gratitude of the donor that he had something to give. The Doll Festival is represented by actual motifs of dolls, the shell-game equipment (Fig. 27), or by peach blossoms. Boys' Day is symbolized by the carp, representing strength and perseverance. The iris is another motif associated with this festival as its leaves represent swords. Tanabata is represented by spindles or looms for weaving, and the Chrysanthemum Festival has, of course, its own symbol.

Since only those with authority could afford embroidery, it is logical that many of the motifs used would come from the everyday life of the upper classes. During the long periods of peace, the typical day of wealthy people would be filled with amusements. Among these was the shell game. Pairs of shells would be painted with corresponding pictures. The shells would be turned upside down, and the challenge was to turn up two that matched. Only the two halves which were originally split apart would fit back together. For this reason the motif of shells became a symbol for marital compatibility, as did the box which contained them, since a girl would take her shells with her when she married.

In the centuries before paved roads, the use of wheeled conveyances was restricted to the members of the imperial court. The depiction of an imperial cart (Fig. 28) in an embroidery raises it to a high level of dignity. To wear a garment decorated with

such a design to any occasion would be seen to bestow honor on the person being celebrated.

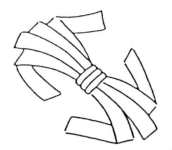

Fig. 26

Fig. 27

Fig. 28

◀◀ Works of literature often furnished inspiration for embroideries. Collection of Jon Eric Riis.

Another favored pastime was the composition of poetry, specifically *renga* or linked verse. In this amusement one person would compose a few lines and the next person would be expected to continue it without long pauses. Poems were written on heavy card-weight paper which had faint designs on the writing side (Fig. 29).

The arrival of the lengthening nights of autumn signaled the time for reading and music, for quiet pursuits rather than outdoor activities. Musical instruments such as the *koto* (or only the bridges that support its strings), drums, flutes, or the *shō*, books, or a lamp by which books could be read or music enjoyed all suggest autumn. The most sophisticated music of court life was that derived from the ancient Chinese court music and dance called *gagaku*. The helmets worn in this dance are called *torikabuto* (Fig. 30), and it was these that came to symbolize the most formal and dignified type of music.

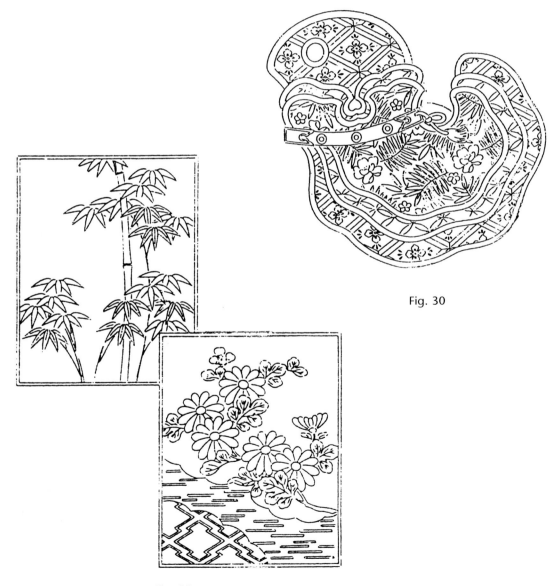

Fig. 30

▶▶ The motif of an overflowing *sake* vessel with a fan in the background is a reference to a mythical comic character called a *shōjō*. This orangutan-like creature, with its love of drink, is a symbol for celebration.

Fig. 29

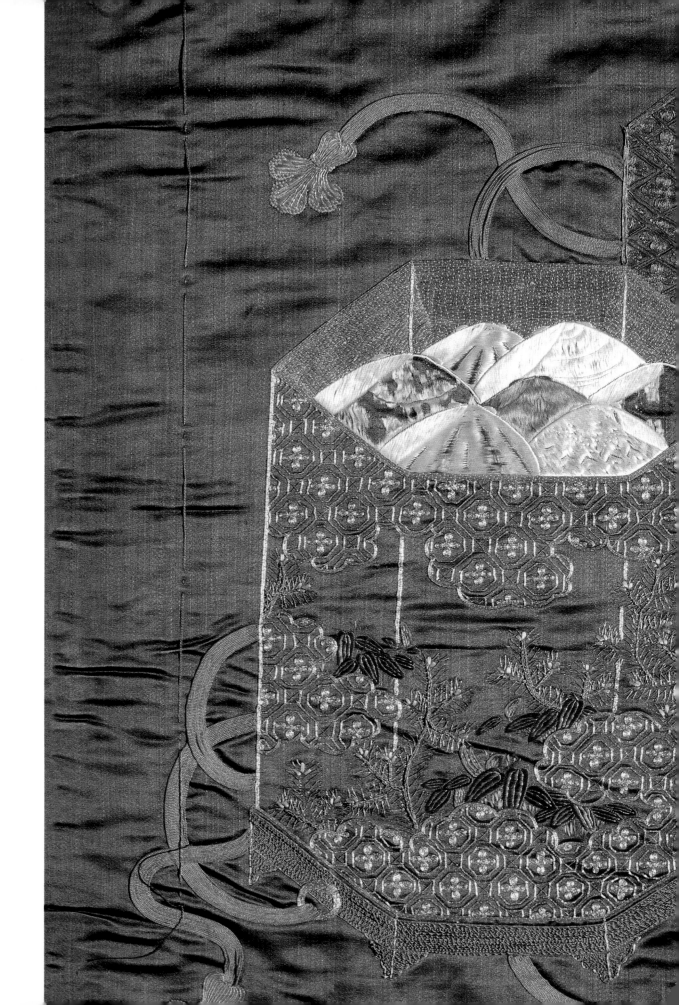

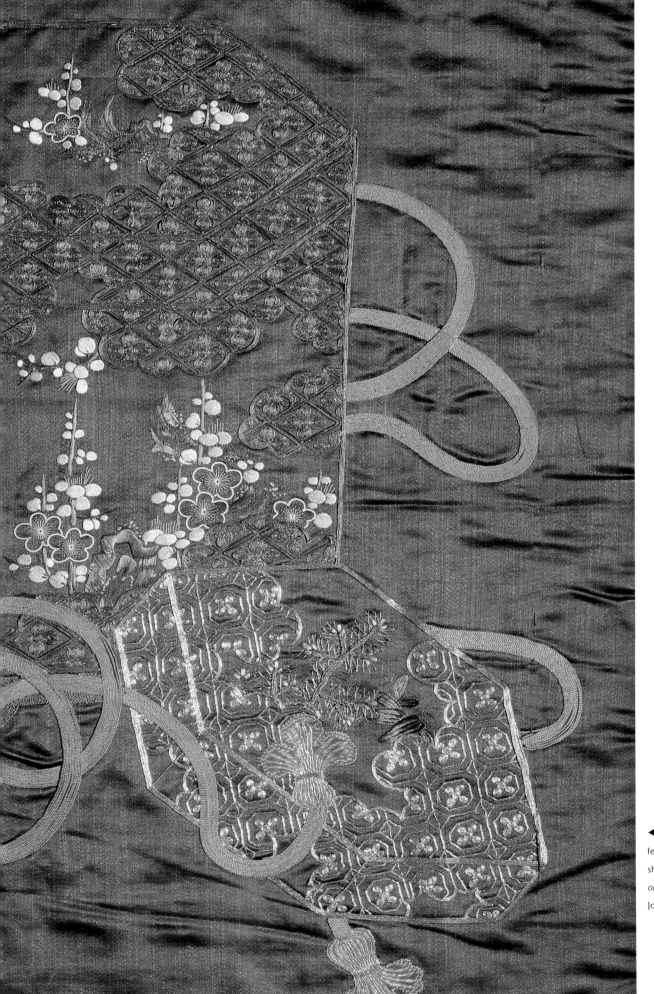

◄◄ Antique *fukusa* featuring design of shell boxes (*kai-oke*). Collection of Jon Eric Riis.

Motifs came also from everyday life, and so clappers for scaring away birds from the maturing rice are appropriate in autumn. *Temari* balls (Fig. 31), made for children's toys, the *buri-buri* (Fig. 32), a pull toy supposed to take away bad luck, and *anesama* dolls (Fig. 33) all appear in embroidery.

Calligraphy is also found as a design motif. In some instances, characters for good luck are used as the design or over the whole design. More recently, characters have been used to replace an element of a design. More than any other piece of Japanese literature, *The Tale of Genji,* a novel written in the eleventh century, has influenced Japanese art, including embroidery.

Contact with the outside world during the Tokugawa era (1600–1868) was limited to trade with a single Dutch vessel permitted to come to Nagasaki once a year. So impressed were the Japanese by this strange and foreign type of vessel, that it became a motif for embroidery, bearing the same connotation as the traditional form.

It is not difficult to see that symbolism forms a vital element of Japanese embroidery. Over the centuries, a language of symbols developed which was pervasive enough to be recognized even by those who could not afford luxury goods. Still today, when the *kimono* has fallen from favor, these designs are known and used by people of every social stratum. Even though Japanese society is known for its homogeneity, the widespread use and understanding of these symbols is still surprising.

Fig. 32

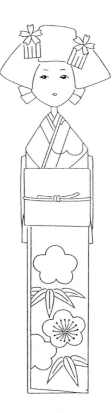

Fig. 33

Fig. 31

▶▶ The four characters (*ka-ho-ha-na*) are used in place of the morning glory blossoms.

■ **THE MOTIFS OF JAPANESE EMBROIDERY** ■

CHAPTER 3

THE EQUIPMENT AND METHODS OF JAPANESE EMBROIDERY

Japanese embroidery requires tools and equipment that are unfamiliar to the western worker. It is only by using these, however, that the necessary tension can be maintained on both fabric and thread, thus creating the unique appearance of Japanese embroidery.

PRINCIPAL FABRICS FOR JAPANESE EMBROIDERY

It is said that silk is the jewel of the world of thread and fiber, as it is certainly among the most expensive textiles. When choosing silk as the fabric for Japanese embroidery, the material must be suitable for both the ultimate use of the completed work and the type of stitching that will be done. Many beautiful fabrics are not suitable for embroidery due to the way they are woven. Some are too spongy, some too soft, many too light in weight. Heavy stitching requires a strong fabric. Over centuries of trials, fabrics that do not work well have been eliminated, and the most appropriate ones have been retained as suitable grounds. In Japanese embroidery a great emphasis is placed on using fabrics, designs, and techniques that are suitable to the season during which the finished products will be worn or displayed. This, too, enters into the selection of fabrics.

The width of all Japanese silk fabric is approximately 13⅜ in, with none under 11⅞ in and none over 15¾ in. The choice of this width is based on the hip size of the average Japanese, so that garments constructed of four segments of this fabric would fit most people. This narrow width is convenient when framed up as the stitcher can reach comfortably to any area to be embroidered. There are only a few exceptions to the 13⅜ in width. Special double-width fabrics are woven to make the *maru-obi*, a luxurious *obi* that is folded in half when worn. Half-width fabrics are used for making the *han-eri* (half-collar) scarves that are worn underneath the *kimono* collar, slightly protruding. Japanese fabrics are sold in rolls, with an *obi*-length roll being 5 yd, while a *kimono* roll is 20 yd long.

When a selvedge is present, which is almost always the case, it is easy to determine the warp and weft directions of the fabric. The warp threads (those set up on the loom for weaving) are parallel to the selvedge, and the weft threads are those for filling. If no selvedge is present, these directions can sometimes be ascertained by pulling gently on the fabric in the line of the threads. The weft threads will have a slightly greater capacity to stretch than the warp threads.

Types of Fabric

In general, *kimono* fabric is thinner and more supple than *obi* fabric, but some fabrics are used for both purposes. The following descriptions are designed to give you basic information. If you are engaged in a course of study, your Japanese embroidery teacher will teach you proper fabric selection.

Habutae *Kimono* lining fabric woven without pattern. It is available in a variety of thicknesses, and only the strongest should be used for Japanese embroidery. It may be dyed in boiling water, in a similar manner to that used for dyeing flat silk thread.

Kimnon-ji This term refers to a variety of weights of fabric suitable for *kimono*. It is woven in an overall pattern, a factor which must be taken into account when determining the suitability of an embroidery design for embellishing the fabric. Since this type of fabric is too thick to be dyed in boiling water, dye is brushed on.

Tsumugi As this fabric is woven with silk harvested from scrap cocoons, it is used for informal costume only. Thin *tsumugi* is used for *kimono*, while thicker

◄◄ A Japanese 'thunder drum' (*taiko*).

weights may be used for *obi*. It is brush-dyed.

Chirimen The most formal *kimono* are made from this silk crepe fabric. It is usually brush-dyed black. Thicker weights of this fabric may be used for *obi*.

Mon-muji *Mon* means 'pattern,' while *muji* means 'no'. This fabric, therefore, has no pattern woven into the background. Thin weights of *mon-muji* are used for *kimono*, but thick *mon-muji* may be used for informal *obi*.

Shioze obi This fabric is woven in such a way as to produce distinct weft valley lines. It has no other pattern woven into the background. It is brush-dyed.

Shusu The thread for this fabric is dyed in boiling water before the cloth is woven. The satin weave produces a smooth, shiny surface, with a soft, yet substantial, texture.

Nishijin-muji *Nishijin* is the district of Kyoto where fabrics have been produced for centuries. *Muji* means 'no pattern'. Usually this type of fabric is used for the back of an *obi*, but it is woven exclusively of thread that is dyed in boiling water first.

Nishijin-haku *Haku* is the Japanese word for gold leaf. In this type of *nishijin*, both vat-dyed threads and gold-leaf strips are used, creating one of the strongest and richest fabrics used for formal *obi*. Many colors of metal leaf may be used to make this type of fabric.

Tsuzure This *obi* fabric is woven of vat-dyed thread and metallic threads together, to make a fabric that is so thick and strong a thimble may be needed to embroider it. The front and back of this fabric are reversible.

Ro Lighter-weight fabrics are used for summer *kimono* and *obi*. In *ro* fabric, a space is left in the weft of the fabric, every three, five, or seven threads, forming horizontal bands. The type of *ro* used for *obi* is thicker and stronger than that used for *kimono*. *Ro* is brush-dyed.

SPECIAL TOOLS AND EQUIPMENT

Spools (koma), used as a pair for laying down non-stitchable thread when couching.

Needles: (a) flat-eyed, hand-made needles in more than a dozen sizes, for stitching with both flat and twisted thread; (b) machine-made needles, for couching thread.

Felt needle-holder, a pad made of oiled felt, to hold needles and give some protection against rust.

Japanese scissors. Japanese embroidery scissors have no finger holes. They are used by simply squeezing them. It is felt that this speeds up the stitching significantly. As with all proper scissors for embroidery, they have narrow blades when one looks at them side-on, so that threads can be clipped closely. Although Japanese scissors are the best choice, small, sharp-pointed western embroidery scissors may be substituted, if desired.

Stroking needle (teko-bari), a tapered piece of tempered steel about 4 in long used to smooth and flatten silk threads. At the end that touches the hand it is squared off to provide a comfortable grip. Because its tapering continues all the way to the tip, without abrupt change, it enables the stitcher to control the thread until the last split second as the stitch is formed.

Awl. The awl used for Japanese embroidery is about 4 in long. It has a wooden handle and a narrow tapered metal shaft that fits and wedges into one of the holes of the frame. It is used for unspooling flat silk threads and for holding them while a twisted thread is being made, as well as tightening lacing thread when attaching fabric to the Japanese embroidery frame.

▶ Special tools and equipment are used for traditional Japanese embroidery.

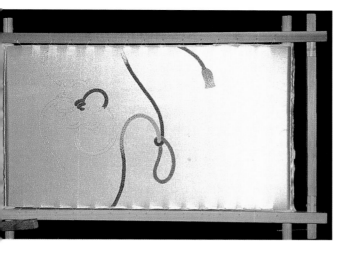

Japanese embroidery is worked on a special frame that holds the fabric drum-taut. This is required to enable the stitcher to pull the silk threads extremely tight, thereby keeping the stitches regular and enhancing the shine on the silk. No other method of framing will produce the same degree of tautness and, at the same time, allow for additional tightening as the fabric relaxes.

The fabric is always mounted on the frame by stretching in the warp direction first. The weft threads are generally softer than the warp threads because the warp threads are harder and firmer (so as to bear the tension of weaving on the loom). If the weft threads are stretched first, minute spaces will open in the fabric, and it will not be as stable once removed from the frame.

◄◄ Japanese embroidery frame.

The first stretching is done between the dowels. Once the fabric has been mounted very tautly and evenly, it is laced firmly to the warp bars (side bars, horizontal bars). Finally additional tension is added in the weft direction by placing pieces of chopstick (or other similar bits of scrap wood) in the cut-out spaces where the weft bars are inserted into the warp bars.

Parts of the Frame
- 2 horizontal (warp) bars with lacing holes
- 2 pairs of shuttle poles (split dowels or half-rounds)
- 2 weft bars
- 2 nails
- chopsticks

Preparing the Fabric for the Frame
When the fabric itself is too short for the frame, attach white cotton additional fabric along the sides (Fig. 1), adding an extra ¼ in seam allowance on both sides of the cotton. (This extra fabric must be 100 per cent cotton and very densely woven.) Stitch the two fabrics together along the weft threads, wrong sides together, and seam allowances on top. Double-stitch the ends of the seam for ¾ in for added strength.

Brush, dish and shell powder: for tracing designs onto fabric. Designs are traced onto stitched foundations or fabric by means of shell powder. This powder is made by finely grinding the shells of oysters, and using the part which yields a white pigment. A fine-tipped, bamboo-handled paintbrush, of the sort used for water color painting, not calligraphy, is appropriate. Mix the powder with water in a small, shallow, white dish.

Small cotton cushion stuffed with cotton: for patting dust out of the embroidery.

Light-weight cardboard lamp: rests directly on the work and can be positioned to give light where needed.

Protective paper: thin, transparent paper, which is rough on one side and smooth on the other. It is used, smooth side down, to protect the surface of the embroidery, and for doing shell-powder transfers.

Finishing paper: heavier than protective paper, very smooth and shiny on one side, and oil-free, for the finishing process.

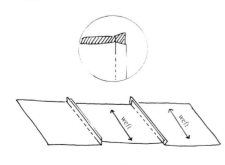

Fig. 1

If the fabric to be embroidered is long enough to reach the shuttle poles (half-dowels or half-rounds), additional fabric may be laid over it for protection as it is wound.

If the fabric has no selvedge, make a line of stitching about ¼ in in from the raw edge of the fabric. Later, the fabric is laced onto the frame, with the lacing inside this stitched line.

Assembling the Frame and Attaching the Fabric

Warp Direction

The warp direction (the direction along the warp threads of the fabric) is stretched first. This keeps the fabric perfectly taut and straight.

① Insert the weft bars into the horizontal bars. Next, insert one half of each pair of half-dowels into the horizontal bars, alongside the weft bars at each end.

② Place each end of the fabric, raw seam edges up, over each half-dowel. After placing the fabric over the bottom half, slide the other half-dowel into place (Fig. 2) so that the fabric is gripped between the half-dowels. The dowels should protrude from the frame by about the same amount at all four corners. Keep the weft direction of the fabric perfectly straight and taut.

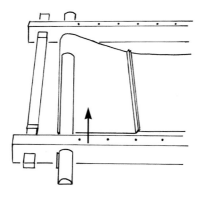

Fig. 2

③ Insert a nail downwards into each pair of dowels (Fig. 3), on the same side of the frame.

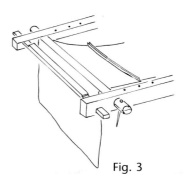

Fig. 3

④ Loosen the fabric by pulling it down in the center, then wrap it around one dowel, rotating it one-and-three-quarters turns in an outward direction. Allow the nail to catch against the weft bar (Fig. 4), with the nail tip outward.

Fig. 4

⑤ Repeat this procedure at the other end of the fabric. The fabric must be centered between the dowels and must be extremely taut.

⑥ Push the horizontal bars up to the edge of the fabric.

Weft Direction

The weft direction is stretched next by lacing the fabric to the horizontal bars. The lacing thread used for Japanese embroidery is a combination of cotton and rayon. It is important not to use a substitute that is too strong. If the framed-up work is accidentally subject to pressure, the thread should break so as to protect the fabric from tearing. The lacing needle is a #3 milliners.

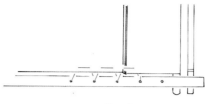

Fig. 5

① Fix the lacing thread to the horizontal bar nearer you by passing the lacing needle through the hole on the extreme right if the silk fabric goes all the way to the dowels, or one hole outside the seam if it does not. Tie the thread firmly around the *inner* side of the horizontal bar (Fig. 5).

② Lace by coming up through the fabric in the middle of the selvedge a quarter of the distance between the hole where the thread is tied and the next hole to the left. Go down through the fabric at a point three-quarters of the distance between the same two holes (Fig. 6). As you work, the right hand is above the frame, the left hand below. This is true for all Japanese embroidery techniques.

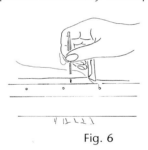

Fig. 6

③ Bring the lacing needle up, eye first, between the selvedge and the horizontal bar, then go down through the next lacing hole (Fig. 7). (Always go downwards when passing through the lacing holes.) Continue this lacing process until you reach the extreme left hole, or one hole outside the seam, on the bar. Bring the thread up between the bar and the fabric.

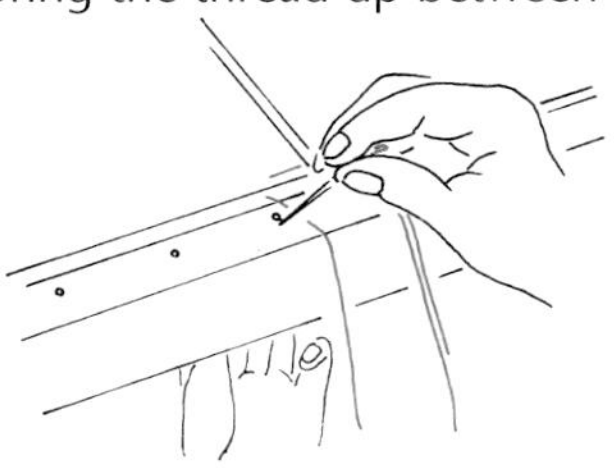

Fig. 7

④ At this point leave the needle on the left side and, starting from the right again, use the awl to pull the laced thread firmly toward the left, always in a diagonal direction, in order to bring the fabric as close to the horizontal bar as possible. Care must be taken not to pull the thread straight but always diagonally, so as not to tear the fabric.

⑤ Finally, pass the lacing thread through the last hole and around the inner side of the bar a few times and tie it there (Fig. 8).

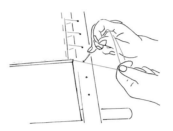

Fig. 8

⑥ Turn the frame around and repeat the lacing process on the other side, working again from right to left.

⑦ The lacing process alone will not produce the necessary tautness in the fabric. To increase the tension, force the horizontal bars farther apart from each other (Fig. 9) and insert small wooden chopsticks in the groove on the weft bars at all four corners. These sticks act as wedges to keep the horizontal bars apart and maintain the tautness of the fabric. Insert them first on the side of the frame with the nails.

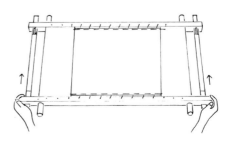

Fig. 9

Double Lacing

If the embroidery is heavy and is expected to take a long time to complete, double lacing is recommended.

① Begin by tying about 2 yd of lacing thread through the first hole where there is part of the design. (It is not necessary to lace the entire length.) Since new pieces of lacing thread can be added when needed, exact length is not critical.

② Pass the needle around the outside of the frame and bring up the eye of the needle in the open space between the fabric and the frame. Take a stitch at the same depth as the ordinary lacing, and immediately bring the eye of the needle back up in the open space (being careful to pass it to the left of the lacing thread).

③ Go around the warp bar (on the outside) and repeat the process halfway between the next holes. Be careful to take this stitch inside (toward the middle of the fabric) the existing lacing thread stitch. Do not split the thread, or it will be weakened. Repeat to the end of the design area.

④ When you run out of lacing thread, tighten the thread with the awl very firmly, and then tie on a new length. Position the knot carefully so that it will not have to be pulled through the fabric.

THREAD TWISTING

Silk is a continuous filament and can reach a mile or more in length when unreeled from the cocoon. In order to unreel the silk, one must kill the silk moth inside. Many filaments are reeled together to form a strand of 'flat' silk. The exact number will vary according to the diameter of the filament. Since it is necessary, for propagation, to allow some silk worms to chew their way out of the cocoons, many cocoons have holes in them. The short thread lengths thereby created still have value, but must be twisted in order to hold them together and give them strength for stitching, or for weaving into cloth. The highest quality of this spun embroidery silk is called 'silk floss'. Even shorter lengths are spun with greater twist and called 'twisted silk' (commonly *soie d'alger*). The shorter the lengths, the greater the number of light-absorbing loose ends there are per inch, thus the silks made of them have less shine than filament silk.

There are several reasons for twisting threads. First, twisted thread is less subject to abrasion, which in garment embroidery is an important consideration. Second, twisted thread provides an interesting contrast to flat silk, gives a different physical dimension, and creates a different feeling. Third, twisting a flat silk thread enhances the shine, by creating additional surfaces for light reflection, much as is achieved by faceting a gemstone.

Basic Process

In making a four into one twisted thread($4 \rightarrow 1$), four flat silk threads are combined (2+2) into one twisted stitchable thread.

① Insert the awl into the lacing hole at the extreme right of the horizontal bar on the far side of the frame.

② Hold the end of the thread with your left hand at a distance of one meter or longer from the awl, while holding the thread tube lightly in the right hand. Unspool the thread away from you, taking the tube around the awl (Fig. 10), bring it back to your left hand, catch hold of the thread, unspool it around the awl once more and back to your left hand. Cut it at your hand, and you have four threads of equal length (two threads doubled round the awl to make four threads).

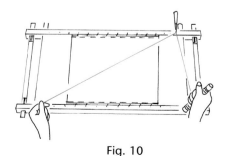

Fig. 10

③ Anchor the threads by looping them over the awl (Fig. 11).

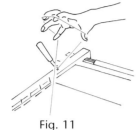

Fig. 11

④ Pass the two threads behind the awl and take two ends in one hand first. Hold the other two ends with your teeth or leave them on the frame (Fig. 12).

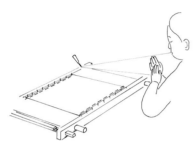

Fig. 12

⑤ Hold the other two ends at the heel of your right hand with the tips of the fingers of the left hand at the height of your right shoulder (Fig. 13). Run your left hand up your right hand (Fig. 14) four times to twist the threads. Pull gently away from the awl, to keep the thread from going slack. Repeat the process with the other two ends, while holding the newly twisted thread in your teeth. This is the UNDERTWIST.

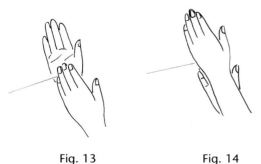

Fig. 13   Fig. 14

⑥ Tie the four ends together (2+2) in the first motion of tying a child's sash or a bow. This will keep the twist from unraveling (Fig. 15). Pull on

each pair of thread ends at the same time to ensure that both threads are exactly the same length from the awl.

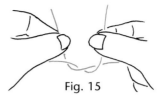

Fig. 15

⑦ Now do the OVERTWIST. Place the two pairs of undertwisted threads at the heel of the left hand at the height of your left shoulder and run your right hand upwards across your left three times, continuing to prevent the thread from going slack. This completes the Z-twist. (An S-twist is the reverse, with the undertwist first on the left then the overtwist on the right.) See Fig. 16.

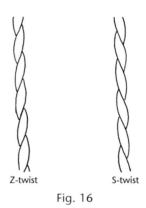

Z-twist   S-twist

Fig. 16

The twist in the two halves of the threads must be the same. Before performing step 6, you may perform a test to compare the twist of each thread half. Keeping tension on the halves between the right hand and the awl, place the left hand in between the right hand and the awl. Move the right hand toward the left hand, and visually compare the twist of the two sides (Fig. 17).

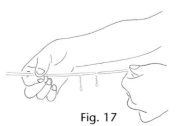

Fig. 17

Twisting Variations

Various non-stitchable threads are used, most generally for edging motifs. If the quantity of thread on each side of the awl is balanced (*karayori*), the effect will be that of a string of small beads. If the quantity is unbalanced (*katayori, boroyori*) the thread will be rippled. Most of these threads are too thick to stitch with.

When only part of a thread is needed, the thread needs splitting. To split a thread, hold one end in the left hand. With either the thumbnail of the right hand or the pads of the fingers, divide the thread into two equal parts. Test that they are equal by inserting the middle finger of the right hand between the two halves and putting tension on the thread over the index finger. Only when the thread is under tension can the relative size of the two parts accurately be determined (Fig. 18).

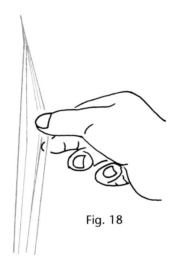

Fig. 18

(4→1) Four (3.5 + 0.5) into one stitchable thread (boroyori)

Split one thread in half. Undertwist three and a half threads four or five times. Twist in the other half-thread when doing the overtwist. This thread, like the basic twist, can be put into a needle for stitching.

(6→1) Six (5.5 + 0.5) into one non-stitchable thread (katayori)

Undertwist five and a half threads, pulling tightly, until they cannot be prevented from kinking. The number of twists will vary from nine or ten twists per yard to forty or fifty twists for a very long thread. Give the other untwisted half-thread 4 in of slack and twist it in while doing the overtwist. The overtwisting should be done some five to ten times less than the undertwisting. This thread should be wrapped around a piece of wood and soaked in water for about three minutes. After it has dried (in the shade), it is wound onto a spool. *Katayori* may be made with many different thicknesses of thread.

(6→1, with gold) Six (5.5 silk and #1 gold + 0.5 silk) into one non-stitchable thread (kinkarami no katayori)

Undertwist four and a half silk threads once or twice, then add a #1 gold thread and undertwist as above. (If the gold thread is twisted in right from the start, it becomes buried among the silk threads.) For the other half-thread and the overtwist, the procedure is the same as for the previous variation (*katayori*).

(6→1, with gold core) Six (5 silk + #1 gold) into one non-stitchable thread (shinkin no katayori)

This is the same as the previous variation (*kinkarami no katayori*), but the gold thread is used for the overtwist. Undertwist the five silk threads until they cannot be prevented from kinking. When twisting in the gold thread on the overtwist, keep it more slack than usual, as gold thread is rather brittle.

(6→1) Six (3+3) into one tight-twist non-stitchable thread (karayori)

Work with three threads first, undertwisting until the thread cannot be prevented from kinking, then do the same with the other three threads. Overtwist the same number of times. Soak and dry, as for *katayori*.

For a smooth *karayori*, as is often used for vein lines, use a soft undertwist and a hard overtwist. While the thread is attached to the awl, run a wet piece of white cotton fabric up and down the thread to dampen it. This thread must be stitched at once before it dries and relaxes. It is generally couched with a 1→2 twisted thread of the same color.

(1➔2) One into two (0.25 + 0.25) and (0.25 + 0.25) thin stitchable thread

Pull one length of thread from thread tube to awl and loop it there to secure it. Separate the thread into two halves of equal thickness. Put one piece aside to be used later. Divide one of these halves into two. Undertwist one quarter, then another; then overtwist them together. Do the same for the remaining half strand, and you have two twisted thin threads.

TRANSFERRING THE DESIGN ONTO THE FABRIC OR STITCHED FOUNDATION

Over the long history of Japanese embroidery, different ways of transferring the design have been used. One of these has been to trace the design onto the fabric using shell powder water and a brush. This requires a certain level of skill. Today more modern methods are often substituted, such as heat transfer or 'prick and pounce'. In this, the design paper is placed on top of a special paper, and a fine needle is used to perforate both layers, creating a pattern. A transfer medium in a color appropriate to that of the fabric is then rubbed through the holes in the pattern paper to apply the design to the fabric.

For guidelines in areas which will be covered by embroidery, shell powder can be painted directly onto the fabric. When a design is to be transferred to a stitched foundation, however, a dry transfer must be made, because the silk threads can soak up too much of the shell powder water if lines are painted directly on the thread. A dry transfer is done by tracing the motif onto the rough side of a piece of tissue (such as is used to protect the work during stitching), and painting on the smooth side. When the transfer is dry, it is applied by holding it in position and rubbing the back of the tissue paper with the flat side of a fingernail. If the lines produced are not completely covered during stitching, they can be removed during the finishing process by beating the embroidery with the velvet cushion.

Never use chalk paper to trace the design, and never use a lead pencil directly on the fabric, to avoid staining the fabric or the embroidery.

① Place a piece of protective paper, rough side up, on top of the design, and trace the design using a pencil.

② Mix a pinch of the shell powder in enough water to make it the consistency of milk (it does not dissolve). Dip the brush into the liquid. (Dip the whole length of the bristles, not just the tip of the brush.) Turn the tracing paper over to the smooth side and, using the wet brush, trace the design with as fine a line as possible. This is easiest if the brush is held vertically.

③ After the design has dried, lay the smooth side of the paper onto the fabric (or stitched foundation) and pin it down on all sides, or hold it carefully.

④ If you pin the paper in place, you can hold a thick flat book or pad against the fabric from below to support it and rub the design onto the fabric with the flat side of your fingernail. An easier method is to place a book which is thicker than the horizontal (warp) bar of the frame on a table. Place the frame on top of the book, and carefully position the paper on top of the fabric. Hold the paper in place with one hand, while you rub the shell powder onto the fabric with the fingernail of the other hand.

⑤ Lift one corner of the tracing paper to check that the design is being transferred to the fabric. Rub more heavily, if necessary.

⑥ Remove the paper and, if necessary, using the brush again, trace over the pattern on the fabric itself. Do not do this on a stitched foundation as too much liquid will be absorbed. By the time you finish your embroidery work, the shell-powder lines will have flaked off, leaving the fabric unsoiled.

WORKING WITH JAPANESE GOLD (OR SILVER) THREAD

Historically, precious metals have been used to enhance embroidery. Once restricted to gold, silver, and their various alloys, the world of metallics has now been expanded to include a wide range of colorful threads. The finest sizes can be stitched if a large enough needle is used to protect the metal from being stripped away from the core. #1 is the smallest size of metal thread which is readily available. In #1 the variations are almost limitless. Brighter and darker colored metallics can be combined with silk or used alone to create a panoply of different effects. Both #1 and #2 may be threaded into a needle and stitched.

Some threads, due primarily to their construction, are not suitable for stitching through the fabric. These must be laid on the surface and couched with a fine thread. Among these are all sizes of Japanese gold or silver above #3, and the hard-twisted threads known as *katayori* or *karayori*. Red or gold-color couching thread is used with gold thread. White or gray couching thread is generally used with silver thread.

Removing the Core from #1 Metallic Thread

When #1 metallic thread is combined with silk in a twisted thread, it is not necessary to remove the core. When it is used in combination with flat silk, however, and often when it is used alone, it is necessary to remove the core in order to allow the metal thread to lie flat. Since this results in a fragile thread, usually a 1-yard length is cut into two for use.

Give about ⅜ in of the thread a sharp twist. The metallic outer thread will separate from the thread core. Hold the core in one hand, and gently push the metallic thread down it. As it bunches, move the accumulated metallic thread down the core. When the metallic thread comes to the end of the core, be sure to push, not pull, it off the core. This is important since the metallic thread is wound like a spring and will stretch.

When the inner core has been completely removed, tidy up the metallic thread by twisting it in the fingers in its natural direction. Finally, holding one end between the thumb and forefinger of one hand, set the twist by breathing heavily on the thread as you restore twist one more time.

GENERAL NOTES ON WORKING EMBROIDERY

- The right hand works above the frame, the left hand below it.

- Keep the needle vertical to the fabric at all times.

- The stitch direction is from top (the side farther away from you) to bottom (the side nearer you) or from right to left.

- Right diagonal stitching proceeds from top right to bottom left, relative to the axis of the shape, using a Z-twist or a flat thread. Left diagonal stitching goes from top left to bottom right.

- The working order is generally from the left side of the figure to the right. This keeps the right hand away from the stitched area.

- Start with the foreground area of the design.

- The working order in a curved shape is clockwise, using either a Z-twist or a flat thread.

- Stitch one point (the width of one needle hole) outward at protruding points along the outline of a figure and one point inward at receding points, to preserve the integrity of the figure.

- Some designs come with a box chart. This is a chart which gives the order in which the technique is worked, the technique symbol, the full name of the technique, the thread with which it is to be worked, and any special notes. In a class situation, the order of techniques may be changed by the teacher.

Starting and Finishing a Thread

Once the thread has been twisted, cut off the end you are holding and thread it into the needle.

Cut the other end of the thread off the awl, make a small knot, then cut off the thread just beyond the knot so as to leave no tail.

Bringing the needle up through the fabric, make a tiny stitch in the weft direction inside the outline of the figure. This stitch is called a pinhead. The knot and this stitch anchor the end of your thread.

When finishing a thread, make two tiny stitches inside the figure. Then, bringing the needle up again for a third time through the fabric or through a completed area, pull the thread taut and snip it just where it comes through. This will anchor the end of the thread firmly.

Maintaining a Uniform Overtwist

When a degree of twist has been selected (hard or soft), it is important to keep the twist consistent while stitching. To maintain a uniform effect, use one of the following three methods.

① After bringing the needle up through the fabric, keep the thread taut and twist the needle in the direction of the twist in the thread (Fig. 19).

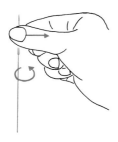

Fig. 19

② Twist the needle while pulling it up through the fabric (Fig. 20).

Fig. 20

③ After the needle goes down again, put your thumb through the loop in the thread and twist the thread itself (Fig. 21).

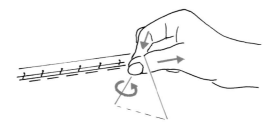

Fig. 21

Embroidering with Flat Silk

Put the entire thread being used through the needle. Do not take half of the quantity of the thread and loop it through the needle.

Keep the thread taut both above and below the frame. When making each stitch, increase tension on the thread by stroking it with the stroking needle.

Move the needle along the underside of the thread from the back of the stitch to the front. Stroke two or three times, *only* in the one forward direction, or the thread will be damaged (Fig. 22).

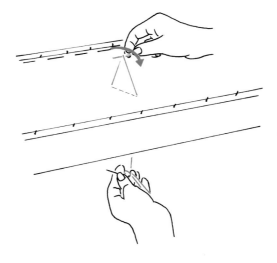

Fig. 22

Embroidering with Stitchable Gold Thread

Fold the thread, put both ends through the eye of the needle, then bring both ends through the loop and close the loop (Fig. 23). This is called a half hitch. It secures the thread so that both strands line up nicely together when sewn. Make a small knot at the end. Stitch with the doubled thread, taking care to prevent it from twisting.

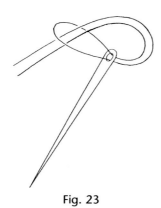

Fig. 23

Techniques for Joining Figures/Motifs

When the motifs to be embroidered touch, the most usual practice is to leave a tiny open area called 'one-point open space'. This makes each motif distinct. Sometimes, however, different procedures are used when a foundation is filled in and there are changes of color, or you want to achieve a heavier textural effect.

① One-point open space
Leave an open space the size of one needle hole (unless the directions call for a wider opening; Fig. 24). To maintain the line of the foreground area, embroider this area first.

② Same needle hole
When stitching through a hole already filled, always go down, so as not to pull the other thread upwards (Fig. 25).

③ Overlapping
Embroider the underlying shape first. When adding

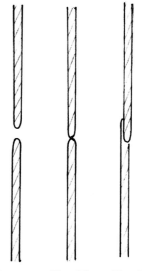

Fig. 24   Fig. 25   Fig. 26

the overlying embroidery, stitch into the underlying thread (Fig. 26).

FINISHING

Most Japanese embroidery over the years has been worked for garments. Since these hang freely once off the frame, it is necessary to stabilize the stitching by pasting the reverse side.

You will need:
wheat starch, cooked into a jelly
old terry cloth towel
wash basin
finishing paper
dry iron (not steam)
small cushion, pure velvet stuffed with cotton

① With the embroidery and frame right side up, check the tautness of the fabric, warp direction first, then weft direction. Check for missing stitches or non-stitchable threads not yet taken to the back (see page 87).

② Turn the embroidery and frame upside down. Snip off all ends of threads to a length about ⅛ in.

③ Turn right side up. Use the velvet cushion to pat any dust out of the embroidery. Pat firmly, while supporting the fabric from below with one hand. Then sweep over the right side of the fabric with the velvet cushion in the weft direction (Fig. 27).

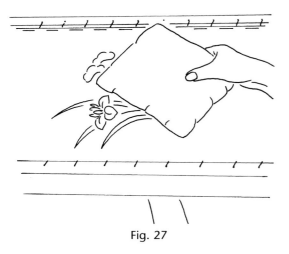

Fig. 27

④ Turn the embroidery and frame upside down. Put a very small amount of starch in the palm of your hand, add a little water, if necessary, and work it into a very thin film. Rub this onto the back of the embroidered areas with your fingertip. Rub in the direction of the embroidery stitches and be careful to stay within the embroidered area so as not to stain the fabric.

⑤ With the embroidery still upside down, wipe the back with a wet towel which has been wrung out well, wiping the starched areas first. Then, using a clean portion of the towel, wipe the whole fabric in the weft direction. This evens out the starched areas and dampens the whole fabric.

⑥ Turn the embroidery right side up, but work from below the frame as follows. Dip the towel in water, wring it a little, fold it into two layers, and place it onto the flat surface of a hot dry iron (the hotter the better). Hold the iron with the towels upside down and close to, but not touching, the back of the embroidered areas until steam comes up through the embroidery. In this way, steam the entire underside of the fabric, working slowly back and

forth in the weft direction. To prevent staining the fabric, neither iron nor towel should touch the fabric directly (Fig. 28).

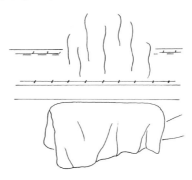

Fig. 28

⑦ Lay finishing paper on the right side of the fabric, with the smooth side of the paper facing the embroidery. With the iron at its lowest setting, move the iron very lightly over the paper in the weft direction. Keep one hand below the fabric to support it and to check on the temperature of the iron. If it is too hot to be comfortable to your hand, allow the

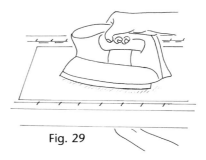

Fig. 29

iron to cool. Do not put pressure on the iron from either above or below. The purpose of this ironing is to enhance the brightness of the threads (Fig. 29).

⑧ Turn the embroidery upside down. Lay the finishing paper on the back of the fabric and iron lightly in the weft direction to dry the fabric. Leave the embroidery on the frame to dry and cool completely for about eight hours. If it is removed while still damp or warm, wrinkles will form.

⑨ To remove the fabric from the frame, reverse the procedure used for assembly: remove the wooden wedges, then the lacing threads, then the nails.

CHAPTER 4

THE STITCHES OF JAPANESE EMBROIDERY

The techniques of traditional Japanese embroidery are described in this chapter, but these descriptions are not meant to replace a teacher. There is no way that the written word can explain the correct tension for your fabric or how your thread should look when it is correctly twisted. Please take every opportunity to work with a trained professional, and use the following explanations as reinforcement.

LAYER OR STITCH DIRECTION

The beauty of traditional Japanese embroidery relies upon its mastery of stitch length and direction. In learning to control stitch direction, it has been found useful to divide the stitches into five groups.

Five letters are used to designate the most basic or fundamental techniques, those which indicate the direction of a foundation layer of stitches, or those which designate the direction of stitches which will form a final layer. They are written with capital letters when abbreviating the name of

the stitch. The word 'into' is symbolized by an arrow pointing to the right ($\rightarrow$), when instructions for a particular technique specify the quantity of thread to be used. For example, $4\rightarrow1$ means four strands of flat silk comprise one stitching thread.

The symbol set is flexible, allowing countless combinations of techniques. For example:

2PsW   **2** layers of **P**adding: **s**titched; the final layer is in the **w**eft direction

C_2tD   **C**ouching: one pair (**2** strands) **t**o and fro in the **D**iagonal direction

Kl/Ra   **K**nots: **l**ong-leg stitched in **R**ealistic: **a**lternating long and short stitches

C_1 + Pc + Bd   **C**ouching: **one** strand; then **P**adding: **c**ouched; then **B**raided: **d**ouble central

The instructions for each stitch are amplified by photographs of that particular technique as used in an embroidered example. The Japanese name for each stitch is given in parentheses after the English name.

◀◀ This *kusudama* (flower ball) design includes all the techniques of Japanese embroidery, and is used as the Phase X (teacher graduation) piece.

W Weft layer (nuki-jibiki)

Make large stitches in lines along the weft (Fig. 1) of the fabric (each stitch being the full width of the figure/motif, or section of the figure being stitched). The stitch direction is from top to bottom, parallel with the weft threads; the working order is from left to right. Keep the threads close together, leaving no spaces between them, so as to lay a solid foundation (see photograph). Be careful to maintain a consistent overtwist in the thread.

At the end of a thread leave a space the width of one thread between the last two stitches. Fill in this space with the first stitch of the new thread.

If this stitch is used on small motifs, it is used as a single layer. If other embroidery is to be worked on top, it forms the weft foundation layer. If it is to be a foundation, temporary holding must be used to secure it.

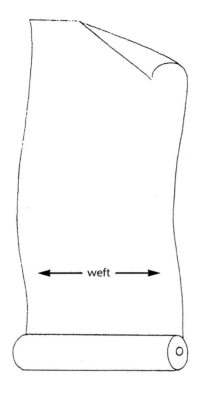

weft

Fig. 1

Temporary holding

After finishing the foundation layer, secure it with temporary holding threads unless some other form of holding is to be used. These threads are laid at ⅜ in intervals at a right angle to the foundation, using 1→2 thread of the same color as the foundation thread (Fig. 2).

Tie these lines down with small stitches spaced at ⅜ in intervals along each line, always stitching through the middle of the foundation threads, never between them, so as not to separate them (Fig. 3). Where the foundation is of mixed colors, any color may be used for the holding threads, but the tie-down threads must be the same color as the foundation. Remove the temporary holding threads after all the overlying figures/motifs are completed.

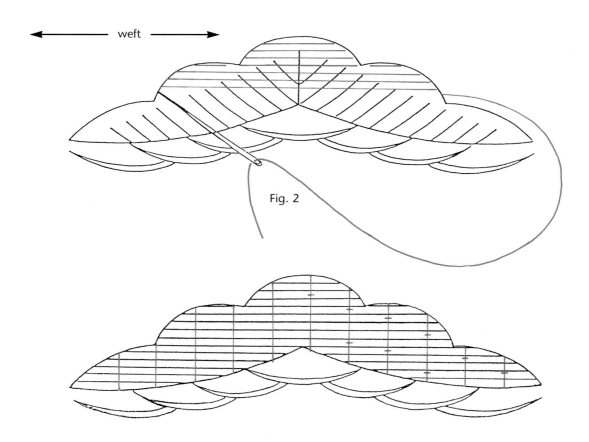

Fig. 2

Fig. 3

H Horizontal layer (nari-jibiki)

Disregarding the lines of the fabric, make long stitches across the full width of the figure at a right angle to its axis (see Fig. 4). Work from the middle of the figure towards the right; return to the middle, and work to the left. The stitch direction is from top to bottom or from right to left. Keep all the lines parallel to the line of the first stitch. After finishing the layer, secure it with temporary holding threads, crossing the foundation threads at right angles and tied down as described in Temporary holding, page 59.

As in weft layers, if the motifs are small, no stitching is placed on top, and the stitch is called horizontal layer. If the motif is large and is to have additional work on top, temporary holding is used, and it is called horizontal foundation layer.

Compared to the weft layer, this horizontal layer gives an impression of movement.

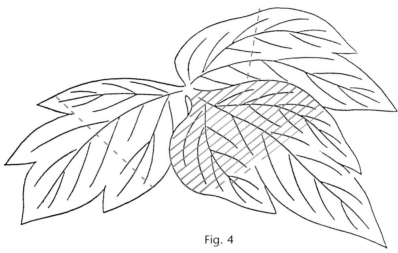

Fig. 4

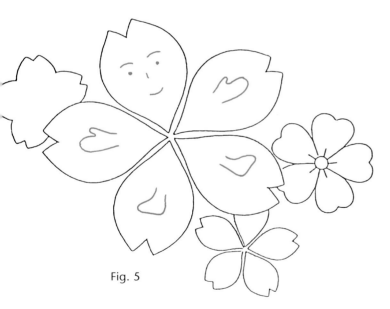

Fig. 5

V Vertical layer (tate-nuikiri)

This is a single layer of stitches along the vertical axis of the figure, used for smaller shapes and motifs, such as cherry or plum blossoms. The embroidery is complete with this one single layer.

The first stitch is in the center of the figure, then work continues first towards the right, then to the left, parallel to the central stitch. Stitch parallel lines, not radiating lines. For the cherry blossom, either flat silk or a soft twist is used, in keeping with the delicacy of the blossom. It is essential for the different parts of the design to be embroidered in the proper order – first the 'face', then the 'arms', and finally the 'feet' (see Fig. 5). The stitch direction is top to bottom or right to left.

At protruding points along the outline of the figure, stitch one point (the width of one needle hole) outward, and at receding points stitch one point inward. This preserves the integrity of the figure (Figs 6–7).

D Diagonal layer (naname-nuikiri)

Diagonal layer is used for regular shapes, such as a curved cord: a single layer of thread is stitched diagonally to the width of the figure.

Begin with an upright stitch along the inner line of the curve and, using right diagonal stitches (from top right to bottom left), slant the stitches away from each other little by little. The working order is clockwise around each curve (Figs 8–10). Use a soft twist in the thread. A filler stitch (Fig. 11) may be used where necessary to avoid leaving open spaces where the ends of stitches fan apart from each other along the outer line of the curve. A filler stitch is an extra stitch more than two-thirds the length of the full stitches. The tip tucks under the previous stitch.

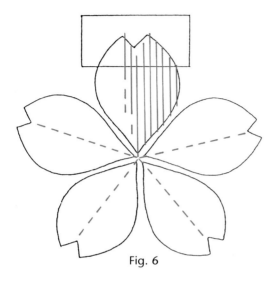

Fig. 6

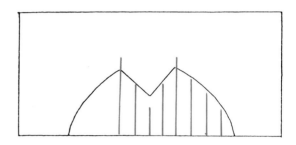

Fig. 7

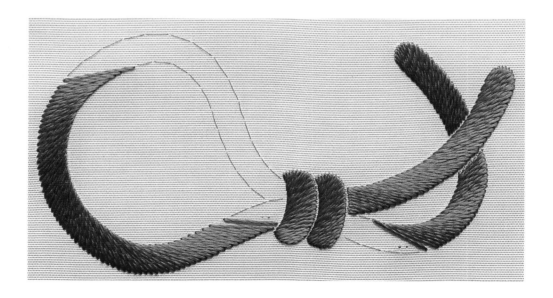

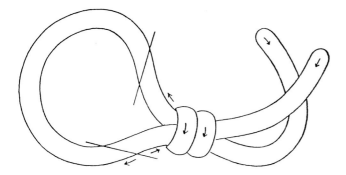

Fig. 8

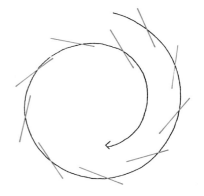

Fig. 9

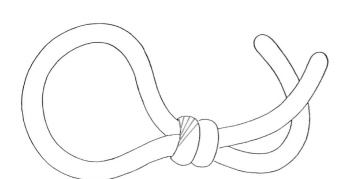

Fig. 10

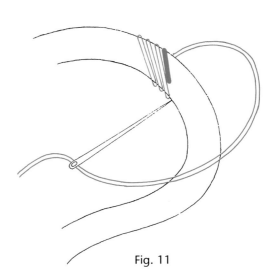

Fig. 11

With irregular shapes, such as chrysanthemum petals, a single layer of thread is laid diagonally across the figure. Note the direction in which the central line of the petal curves and fill clockwise along this curve (Figs 12–13). This means that for some parts of the design you will begin from the tip of the petal and for other parts you will begin from the innermost part of the petal at the center of the flower.

Begin with a straight stitch along the outline of the figure and slant little by little, using a right diagonal. Use filler stitches when needed, but try to

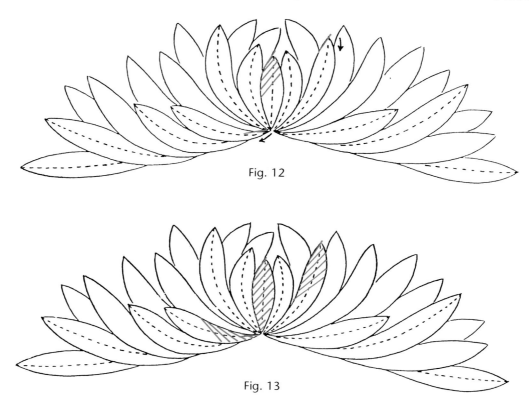

Fig. 12

Fig. 13

avoid them when using flat silk. Stitch one point outward at protruding points along the outline of the figure to sharpen the line.

S Separated layer (wari-nui)

This technique is used for motifs with a central line of separation, such as a leaf pattern or a feather.

Using the central vein of each section of the leaf as a dividing line, start on the concave side of the vein, and work to the tip, with one point outward at the outermost point, then down the other side, leaving a one-point open space to mark the vein. Stitch the largest section of the leaf first, then each smaller one in turn (Fig. 14).

Fig. 14

HOLDING

Hd Holding: diagonal (hippari-osae)

This technique, used only on a foundation of twisted thread, holds the foundation down by covering it with thinner threads stitched diagonally to the lines of the foundation. It is used especially when an elaborate superimposed design will be added over the entire foundation.

These stitches are made in the general direction of the twist in the thread. Adjust the angle until the thread is least visible, and, using 1→2 twisted thread, stitch lines diagonally across the whole surface of the foundation at ⅛ in intervals (Fig. 15). Tie down one line at a time with stitches in the same direction as the foundation threads at ⅛ in intervals. Come up and go down in the middle of the foundation threads from top to bottom, beginning on the left (Fig. 16).

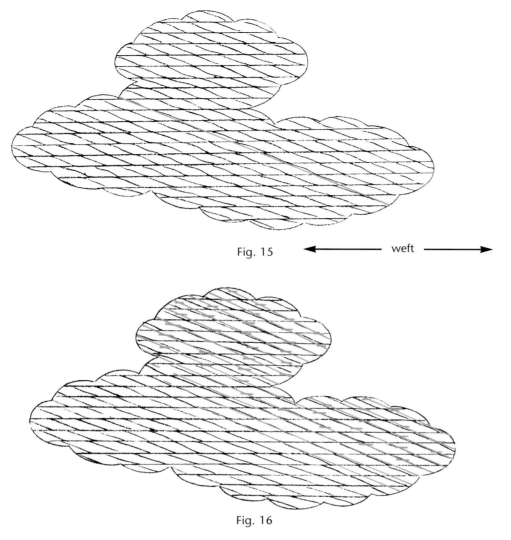

Fig. 15   ◄——————— weft ———————►

Fig. 16

HI Holding: lattice (goban-osae)

This technique, decorative in itself, holds down a foundation of flat thread by covering it with a lattice design of thin threads.

Using a 1→2 twisted thread, stitch the lines at a forty-five degree angle to the foundation threads at ⅛ in intervals, according to the design (Fig. 17). Tie down the threads with one stitch at each intersection. The tie-down stitches are taken in the direction of the foundation layer, working from top to bottom, and filling from left to right (Fig. 18).

This lattice design is itself the decoration and no other layers are superimposed.

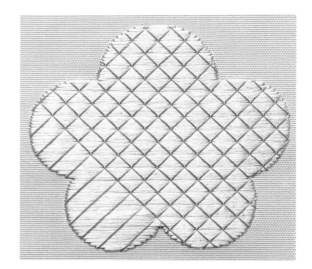

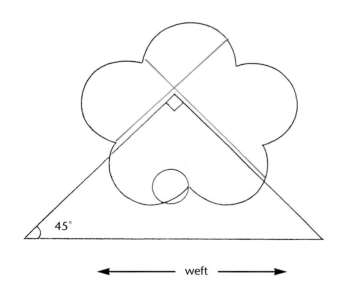

45°

weft

Fig. 17

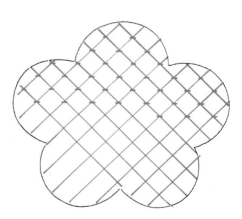

Fig. 18

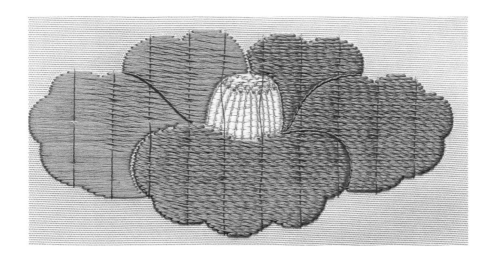

Hs Holding: short-stitch (kiri-osae)

This technique, used on either a twisted or a flat foundation, holds the foundation and creates a delicate color contrast.

Use temporary holding threads (see page 59) at ⅜ in intervals for guidelines. Each stitch of short stitch holding is ¼ in long and holds down three foundation threads at a right diagonal. Stitch through the foundation threads, not between them, so as not to separate them. Stitch from top to bottom and work from left to right. After finishing the first row across, go back to the left and begin the second row at a point half way down the length of the stitching of the first row, and so on (Fig. 19).

On a flat foundation the stitches may be longer and steeper.

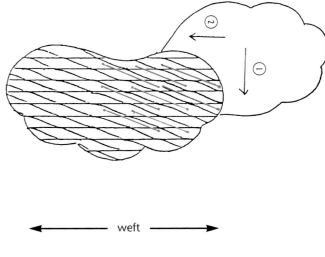

weft

Fig. 19

Lh Line of held thread (hippari-toji)

This simple technique depicts straight or curved lines
with a single or double line of thread.

Stitch a single thread, or two threads to be
gathered into one, along the design line. Use just
enough widely spaced couching stitches to keep
the thread in place (Fig. 20), then tie down the
line (Fig. 21).

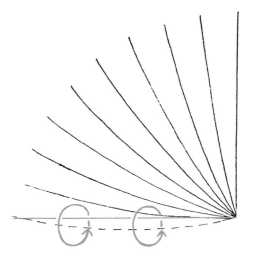

Fig. 20

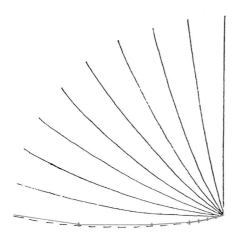

Fig. 21

Veins (yōmyaku-kake)

Veins in a leaf are depicted by adding straight or curved lines of thread. Stitch a thread in a straight line, adding just enough holding to keep it in place (Fig. 22), then tie it down.

If one thread does not adequately fill the space, especially toward the central part of the leaf, add another thread along part of the length, and couch it with the main thread (Fig. 23).

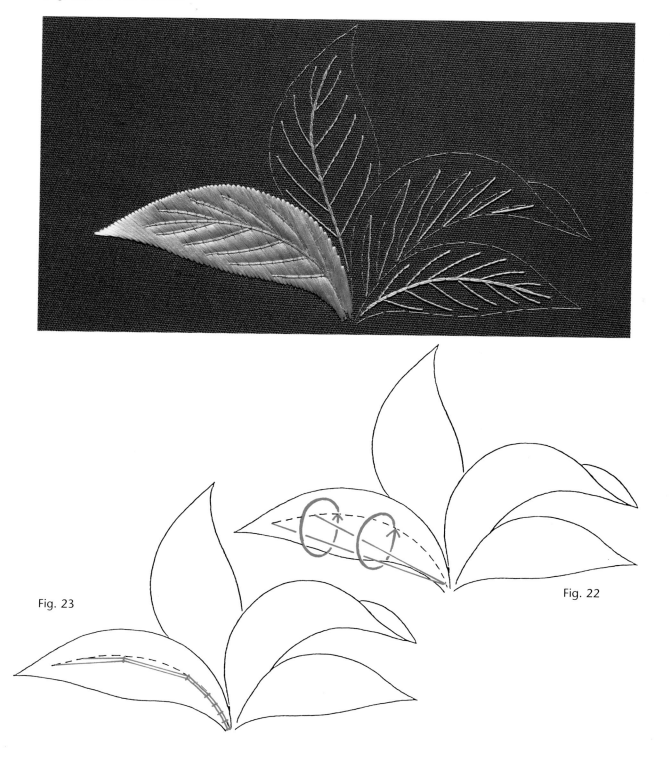

Fig. 23

Fig. 22

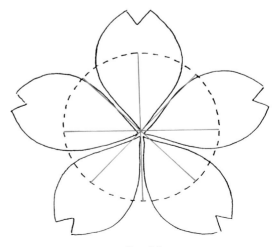

Fig. 24

Fig. 25

Stamen (shibe-kake)

Radiating and circular lines of held thread are used
inside a flower to represent stamens.

First draw the circle of the stamens on thin
paper, go over the line with shell powder, and
transfer it onto the embroidery.

Bring the needle up through the line of the
circle in the middle of the uppermost ('face') petal,
and stitch the thread vertically across the center and
into the line of the circle directly opposite at the
bottom half of the design. Do the same thing across
the horizontal diameter of the circle (Fig. 24). Next,
bisect each quarter-circle by stitching threads across
the center again, this time in an X pattern (Fig. 25).
Again bisect each resulting area, so that you finally
have sixteen lines radiating out from the center of
the circle.

Using a small X-stitch, gather the intersecting threads together and anchor them down at a point slightly below the actual center of the circle (Fig. 26). Tie down each stamen with regularly spaced stitches, beginning with the one halfway between the center of the flower and the end of the thread. Only the central line in the 'face' petal should be straight. All the other lines curve away from this central line. The center line in the bottom half of the design may curve in either direction.

The pollen on the stamen (Fig. 27) may be depicted by two stitches along the outer circle at the end of each radius or by using single round knots (see page 110).

Fig. 26

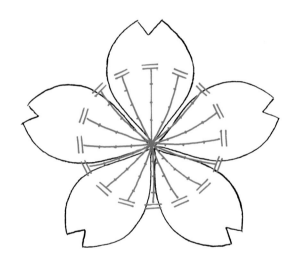

Fig. 27

Ls Line of staggered diagonals (matsui-nui)

In this technique, a line is created by embroidering along the contour of the design using staggered diagonal stitches. This creates a softer effect than that made by a line of held thread. There are two methods: three-stitch (Fig. 28) or four-stitch (Fig. 29). If a thicker line is needed, use diagonal layer (see Fig. 30).

The three-stitch method begins with a half-length stitch, followed by a full-length stitch. Subsequent stitches are full-length, and go one half stitch beyond the previous stitch. The stitching is on the right diagonal traveling in a clockwise direction around any curve.

The four-stitch method begins with a one-third length stitch, then a two-thirds length stitch, then the full-length stitch. Each stitch thereafter extends one-third beyond the length of the previous full stitch, again on the right diagonal stitching and in a clockwise direction around any curve.

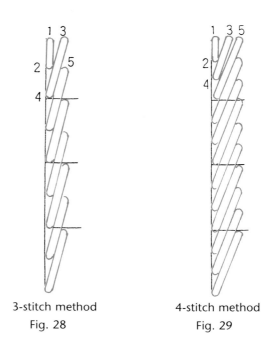

3-stitch method
Fig. 28

4-stitch method
Fig. 29

Fig. 30

GEOMETRIC EFFECTS

Geometric effects, such as Gt (Geometric tie-dye effect) or Gf (Geometric flax-leaf effect) are worked with great regularity and accuracy by using a triangle and measuring with care. Tie-dye effect imitates the *kanoko* (dapple or fawn-dot) tie-dye used in much Edo period costume. Flax-leaf effect creates a flower pattern. Countless other geometric effects can be devised using a compass and ruler. These techniques are generally not considered to be very formal, but nonetheless enjoy great popularity. There are countless possibilities for geometric effects, a few of which are suggested here.

Gt Geometric: tie-dye effect (hitta-gake)

On a foundation layer of white flat silk, stitch lines of colored thread at a forty-five degree angle to the foundation threads and at ¼ in intervals to form a lattice pattern (Fig. 31). Using the same colored thread, tie down the threads at each intersection with a fairly long stitch and add another stitch of the same length on each side of the first. Stitching proceeds in the weft direction, from top to bottom, and the lines of stitching are worked from left to right across the figure (Fig. 32).

When this is complete, put a 'sleeper' stitch in the middle of each open space, and cover with two stitches, shorter than those at the intersections. (When embroidering over a foundation but in the same direction as the foundation threads, a sleeper stitch is first added perpendicular to the foundation threads (like a sleeper, or cross-tie, on a railroad bed) to keep the embroidered stitches from being buried among the foundation threads. The sleeper stitch is shorter than the width of the threads it supports.) Stitch in the weft direction, top to bottom, and work from left to right across the figure. Maintain a consistent twist in the thread throughout.

Finally, to hide the stitching holes along the outermost edge of the figure, a non-stitchable thread, along with a #4 gold thread to frame it, may be couched along the edge, using the couching technique for a pair of gold threads shown on page 87.

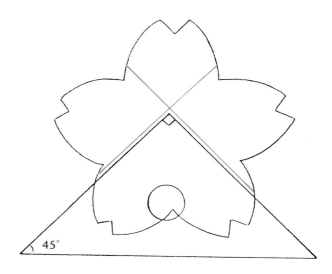

Fig. 31

Fig. 32

Tie-dye effect in relief (hombitta-gake)

To show the tie-dye effect in sharper relief, some of the open spaces of the lattice pattern around the edges of the figure may be filled in (Fig. 33). After stitching the lattice lines, use a 1→2 twisted thread to tie down the intersections of the incomplete spaces with one stitch only, as shown in the instructions for lattice holding (see page 68). Using the same thread you will use for the complete spaces, fill in the left-over areas and add short-stitch holding (see page 69). Once you have finished this, proceed to the stitching of the intersections and centers of the complete spaces, as for geometric tie-dye effect.

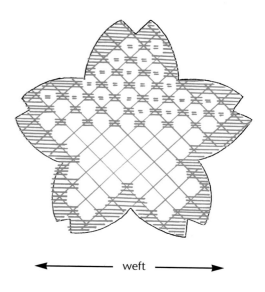

←——— weft ———→

Fig. 33

Gf Geometric: flax-leaf effect (asanoha-gake)

This linear technique adds a pattern of a flax-leaf six-pointed star.

Flat or softly twisted thread of a light, subdued color is used for the foundation. Over this foundation stitch perpendicular lines at ¼ in intervals using either flat or twisted silk (Fig. 34). Next stitch diagonal lines at the angle shown in Fig. 35 and again at the angle shown in Fig. 36. At this point tie down all the intersections with 1→2 twisted thread (Fig. 37).

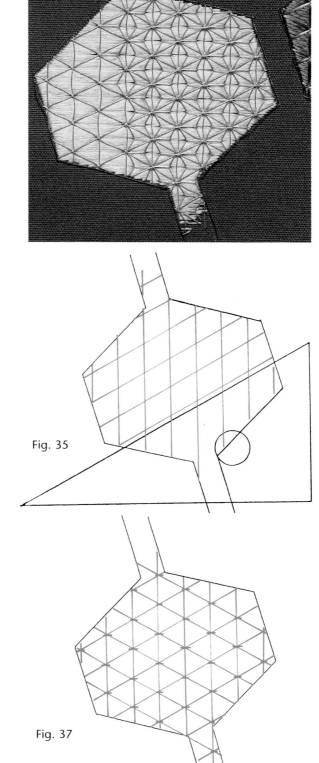

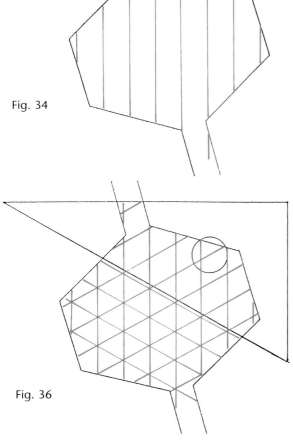

weft

Fig. 34

Fig. 35

Fig. 36

Fig. 37

Finally, divide all the triangular areas into equal thirds using a horizontal stitch pulled upwards or downwards and anchored by a vertical stitch as in Figs 38 & 39. Note that the stitch actually emerges from the corner of the adjacent triangle, resulting in a criss-cross pattern at each of these intersecting points. The thread for this last step may be twisted or flat silk, and a change of color adds an interesting touch.

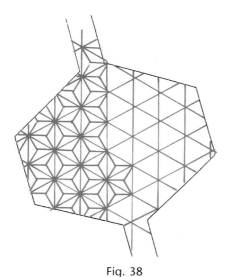

Fig. 38

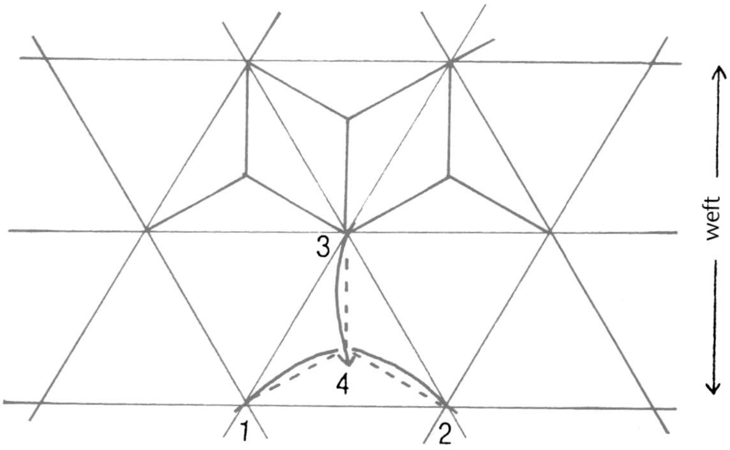

Fig. 39

SUPERIMPOSED PREPARATION

The single aspect of Japanese embroidery that most distinguishes it from other forms of embroidery is the use of superimposed work, that is, stitching on a stitched ground. There are three ways to prepare the foundation for this superimposed work. The first is to trace a linear design on thin paper, the second is to glue and sew down shapes over which the stitching is done, and the last is the use of shell powder and thread, both stitchable and non-stitchable.

St Superimposed: transparent paper preparation (uwamoyō–hippari-toji)

Trace the pattern onto thin, crisp, transparent paper. Lay the paper over the foundation and secure it in place with basting thread or pins. Stitch the lines by sewing through the paper, the foundation, and the fabric. Then tear away the paper. After removing the paper, couch down each line (Fig. 40).

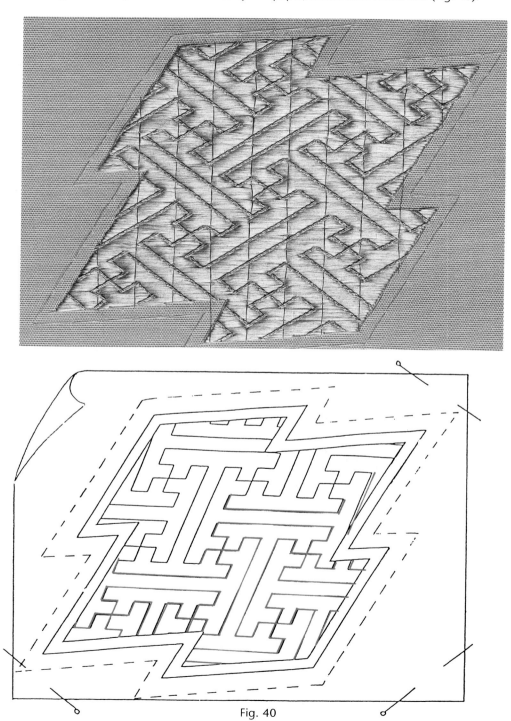

Fig. 40

Sc Superimposed: cut paper preparation (uwamoyō-nuki-nui)

Trace the pattern onto a piece of paper. The paper should be neither as thin as tracing paper, nor as thick as cardboard. Cut the paper a tiny bit smaller than the pattern. Paste the paper lightly into place on the foundation. Stitch around the edge, with stitches which come up in the foundation and go down into the paper. In this case, it is better not to take a stitch at the point of the *shippo* shape. This paper will serve as padding and support as well as being a guide for the outline of the superimposed areas (Fig. 41).

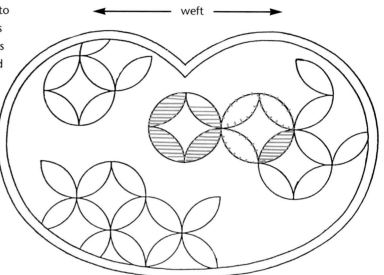

Fig. 41

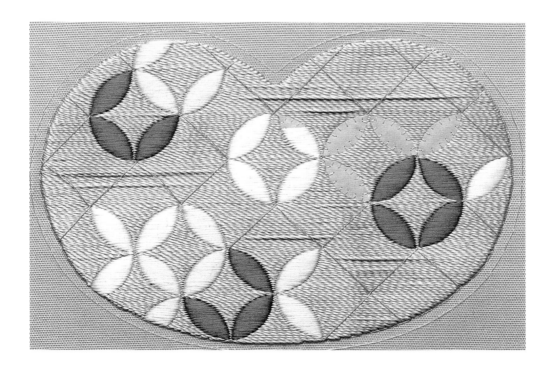

Ss Superimposed: stitched preparation (uwamoyō-nuikiri)

Draw the pattern on the rough side of a sheet of protective paper, go over the lines with shell powder on the smooth side. Transfer the design onto the foundation layer (see page 51). (Do not draw directly onto the threads with the brush, as the threads will absorb the powder and be stained.)

If the outline of the shape is complex, work it with 1→2 twisted thread, making tiny close running stitches. If the outline is fairly straight, using a 1→2 twisted thread, tie down a single line of thread along the outline of the design. The color of this line may be either that of the foundation or that of the thread to be superimposed. The stitches of the superimposed layer will cover this outline, which thus serves to sharpen the edges of the superimposed design and to set it in relief against the foundation layer. The outline also supports the superimposed stitching (Fig. 42).

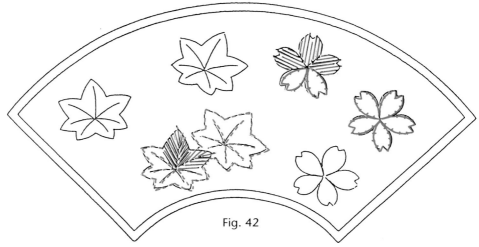

Fig. 42

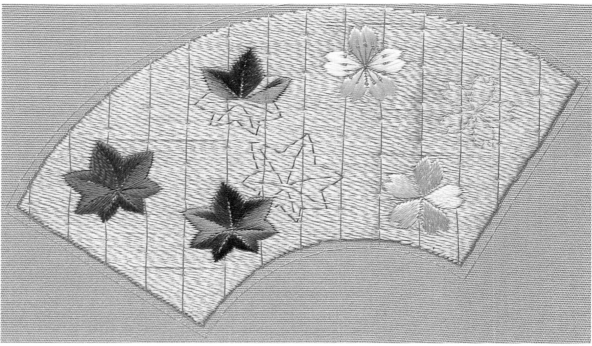

COUCHING

Couching is the technique of holding down a non-stitchable thread (that you wish to be visible) by using another, much finer, thread. When the primary thread is gold, the most usual choices of couching thread are red or gold. When the thread is silver, a gray or white couching thread is most commonly used. Many beautiful and very subtle effects can be achieved, however, by using other colors. In all

This embroidery, featuring a treasure ship motif, is worked using every size of metal thread, and all the major couching techniques.

cases, the color of the couching thread affects the overall appearance of the metal thread but is not highly visible. As the metal thread travels back and forth across the surface of the work, the couching stitches not only hold the thread in place, but also

can be used to change the direction of the thread. The following examples show the correct placement of stitches when turning oblique, acute and right-angled corners (Figs 43–45).

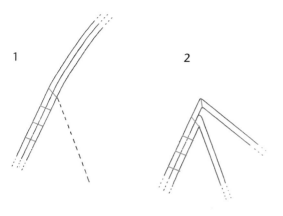

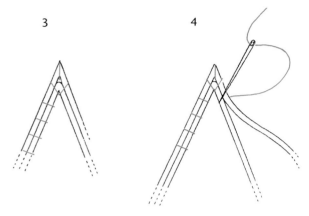

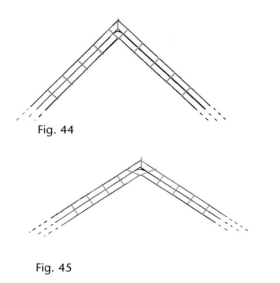

Fig. 43

Fig. 44

Fig. 45

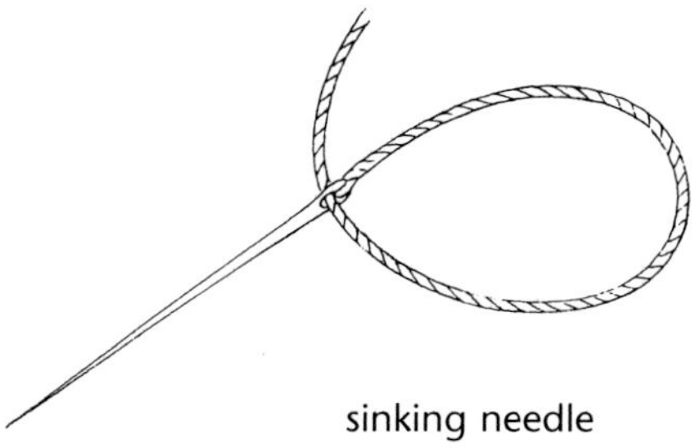

Fig. 46

sinking needle

To finish off when couching a non-stitchable (metal) thread, the ends are pulled down through the fabric using a sinking needle. To do this, first cut the ends of the couched thread so as to leave only ⅛ in. To make a sinking needle, thread a needle with about 15¾ in of silk and bring the needle to the mid-point of the silk thread. Pin the needle securely into the additional fabric with the point toward yourself. Twist first one side of the silk, then the other, holding one end in the teeth while twisting the other. Twist the two strands together into one, then pass the end of this twisted thread through the eye of the needle and pull it almost all the way through so as to leave only a small loop (Fig. 46). Use this loop to catch the ends of the non-stitchable couched thread and pull them down through the fabric one by one (Figs 47–48). The silk thread may be reinforced by rubbing in a small amount of natural glue or wheat paste.

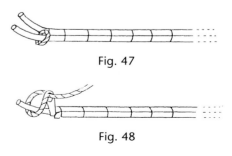

Fig. 47

Fig. 48

C₂ Couching: one pair (2 strands) (komadori ikkai)

Two spools are generally used together as a pair when laying down (couching) lines of non-stitchable thread. The threads are laid in a clockwise direction.

Leaving ⅜ in at the end, couch the end of the first thread (Fig. 49).

Lay the end of the second thread next to the first, then with the second couching stitch directly over the first stitch, couch both threads together. This holds them firmly in place (Fig. 50).

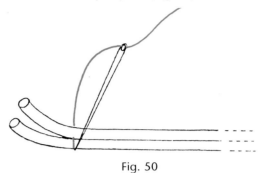

Fig. 49

Fig. 50

Continue to couch the pair at every second twist along the thread (Fig. 51), taking a single stitch over both threads. The stitch direction is right to left or top to bottom.

After the needle passes below the frame to the left hand, line up the spools and tug them with the right hand while pulling the couching thread down with the left. Gold and silver threads have a special beauty when pulled taut. This also stops the threads from loosening when the fabric is removed.

C$_4$ Couching: two pairs (4 strands) (komadori nikai)

A second pair of threads is laid down to the right or to the inside of the first pair, leaving no space between the two pairs. (For instructions about laying down the first pair see page 87.) The second pair is couched at points half-way between the couching of the first pair. From the brick-like effect that it gives, this is called,'brick couching' (Fig. 52).

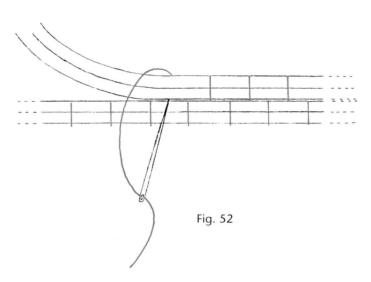

Fig. 52

C$_3$ Couching: one and a half pairs (3 strands) (komadori ikkai-han)

A single thread, from only one spool, is laid down next to the first pair of threads and is couched with the closer thread of that pair at points halfway between the previous couching (Fig. 53).

Fig. 51

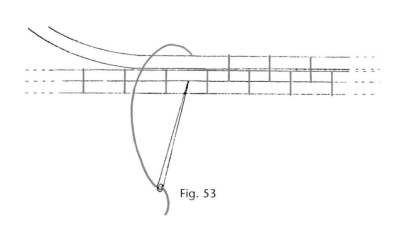

Fig. 53

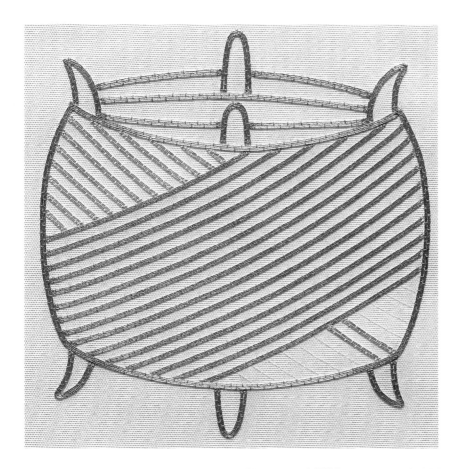

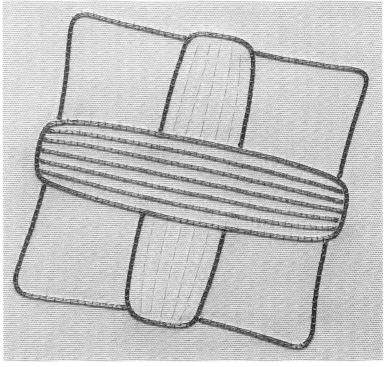

C$_1$ Couching: single thread (1 strand) (komadori-katakoma)

Lay down a single thread and couch it. At very steep angles, couch the outer tip of the angle first, then, with the next stitch, couch across the point, where the thread is double thickness, then continue across the single thread (Figs 54–55).

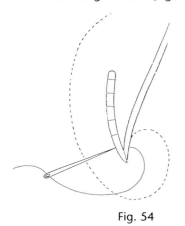

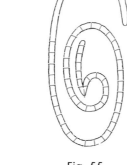

Fig. 54　　　　　　Fig. 55

C$_2$r Couching: one pair (2 strands) round and round (hiraume-hakoume)

This technique is a continuation of couching: one pair. One pair of threads goes round and round until the area of the figure is solidly filled.

Work from the outside of the figure inwards, clockwise around the figure. After finishing the outline of the figure, continue around within the previously laid threads. Lay the threads down closely together, turn corners properly, use C$_2$ brick couching (see page 87), and pull the ends down through the fabric (Fig. 56). (Note that the couching thread at the angles forms interesting lines of color within the figure.)

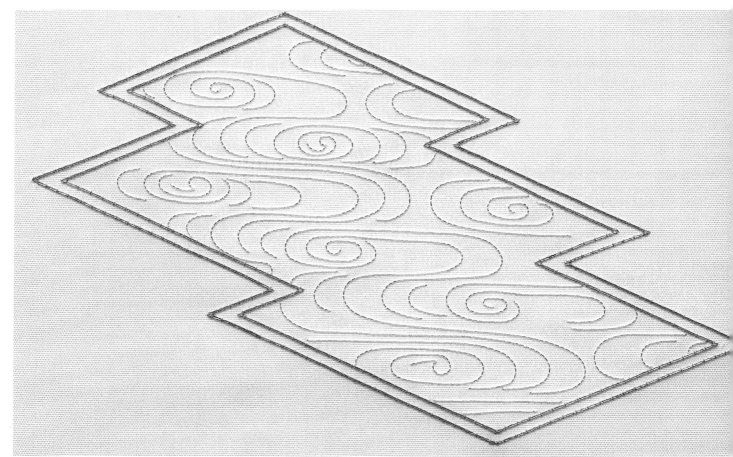

C$_2$t Couching: one pair (2 strands) to and fro (hiraume-hikikaeshiume)

This is a technique for filling up a regularly shaped area. Using one pair of threads, fill up the area by laying lines to and fro. Turn the corners sharply left to right (Fig. 57). Use C$_2$ brick couching (see page 87).

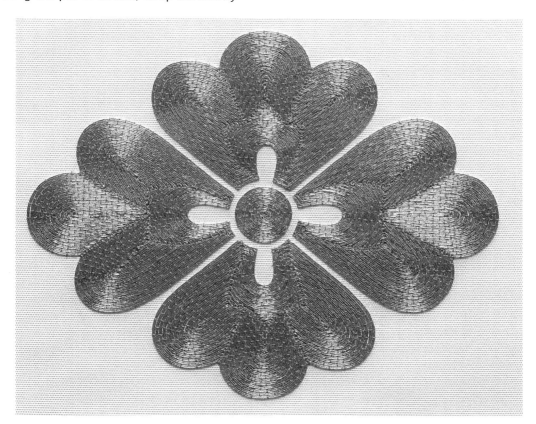

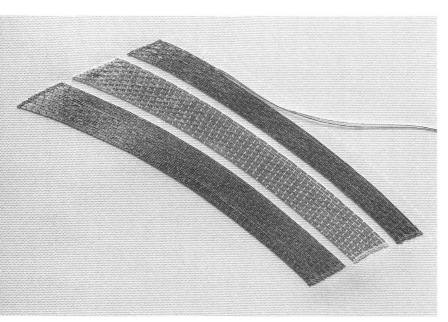

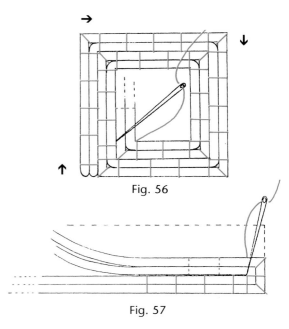

Fig. 56

Fig. 57

C₂o Couching: one pair (2 strands) outward coil (hiraume-tamaume)

This technique is used to fill up a solid round area. Begin with a single thread (end pulled down through the fabric) which, couched at close intervals, coils clockwise around itself until it reaches a diameter of about ⅛ in (Fig. 58). Add another single thread on the outside (end pulled through), and the pair of threads continues to coil outward until the area is filled (Fig. 59). At the end, the inner thread is pulled through the fabric first. The outer thread is then couched with the adjoining thread several times, then its end is also pulled through.

Stagger the couching stitches, but do not line them up into a neat brick pattern, or the intervals between couching will become larger and larger as the threads coil away from the center (Fig. 60).

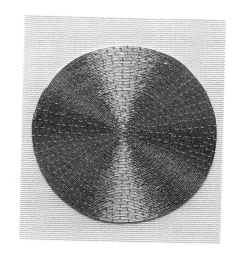

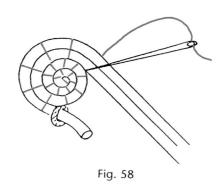

Fig. 58

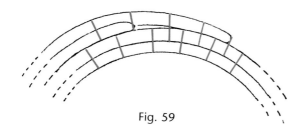

Fig. 59

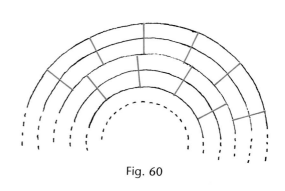

Fig. 60

C$_2$i Couching: one pair (2 strands) inward coil (hiraume-waume)

This technique is used to fill up a round area open at the center, such as a ring. Draw the outside line of the ring with a compass. Begin laying down a single thread (end pulled through) along the outer line of the figure, working clockwise, and, after several couching stitches, add another thread on the inside (end pulled through), and work with the pair clockwise around the figure, with brick couching (Fig. 61).

When the shape is filled, pull through the end of the inner thread first. (The 'inner' thread here is the thread which lines up against the previously laid pairs of thread.) Then continue with the other thread, couching it with the adjoining thread several times and finally pulling the end through (Fig. 62).

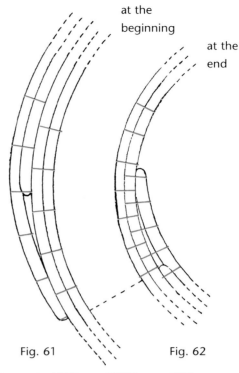

at the beginning

at the end

Fig. 61   Fig. 62

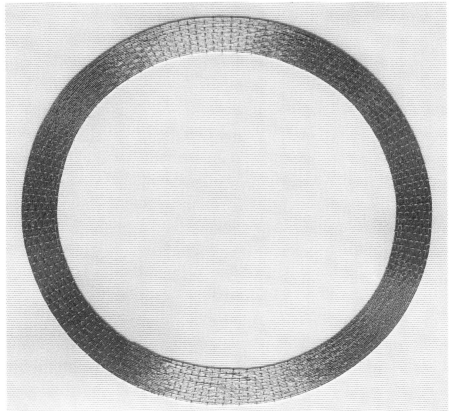

C₁t Couching, single thread (1 strand) to and fro (orandagaeshi)

This is a technique for filling up an irregularly shaped solid area using a single strand of metal thread. The look it creates is flatter and smoother than C_2r.

C₁tW Couching, single thread (1 strand) to and fro, weft direction (nuki-orandagaeshi)

The figure is filled along the weft direction of the fabric (Fig. 63). Using a single thread, begin at the left side of the figure at the bottom. Pull the end through the fabric, then unspool the thread up (away from you), couch it at the outermost point of the figure and bring it back towards you, leaving no space between threads. Couch the downward traveling thread with the preceding upward traveling thread as a pair, using brick couching. Continue to lay the thread up and down, in this manner, until the figure is filled.

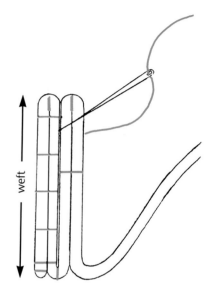

Fig. 63

C_1tD Couching: single thread (1 strand) to and fro, diagonal direction (nuikiri-orandagaeshi)

When the lines are laid diagonally to the weft of the fabric with lines of unequal length, a sense of roughness or movement is conveyed. Work from the left to the right (or clockwise along curves): Figs 64–65. The edge of the figure can be padded, using couched padding (see page 105).

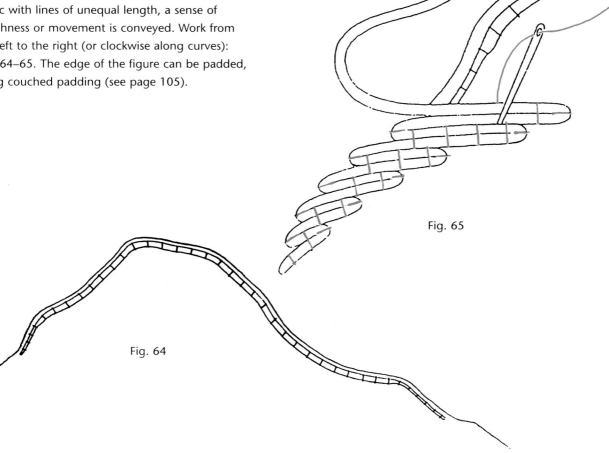

Fig. 65

Fig. 64

C_1tH Couching: single thread (1 strand) to and fro, horizontal direction

To work this technique, a single strand of thread is couched first at one side of the frame then at the opposite side, and is then brought back to lie alongside itself. The pair of threads is couched as one in a bricking pattern (or whatever pattern is desired). For C_1tH the direction of the threads is horizontal to the figure.

C_1tV Couching: single thread (1 strand) to and fro, vertical direction

This variation is worked in the same manner as C_1tH, but the direction of the threads is vertical to the figure.

C_1M Couching: single thread (1 strand), maze (charaume)

This technique fills an area with evenly spaced lines. The effect is light and airy, compared with the solidity of one pair of threads couched round and round.

After laying the outline of the figure with one pair of threads, cut the inner thread and pull the end through. With the other thread continue to lay a single thread line always at the same interval from the previously laid line. Work clockwise around the figure and progressively inward to the center (Fig. 66).

This technique can be superimposed on a weft foundation layer of flat silk.

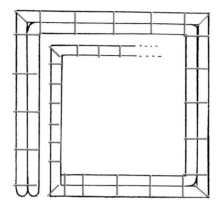

Fig. 66

NOVEL EFFECTS

Novel effects can vary widely, but are sometimes worked as regularly as geometric effects. Blister effect is useful for small flower parts. Woven effect, worked in flat or twisted silk, adds texture, while three-dimensional effect adds depth. There are countless novel effects which can be achieved, a few of which are described here.

Nt Novel: three-dimensional effect (masu-nui)

This technique conveys a three-dimensional feeling through the use of the lattice pattern and color gradation. Using a white pencil, draw the guidelines for a lattice pattern at forty-five degree angles to the weft at ¼ in intervals, right onto the fabric itself.

Using flat silk thread, stitch diagonal lines, two adjacent lines at a time, first in one intersecting direction, then the other (Fig. 67). Repeat, using slightly lighter value thread color with each layer, until the open areas are filled (Fig. 68). The final layer is #1 gold, half hitch (see page 54): Fig. 69. Tie down the uppermost intersections with two stitches along the weft (Fig. 70).

Hide the stitching holes along the outermost edge of the figure by couching one or more pairs of #4 gold or silver thread. Use brick couching if you add more than one pair.

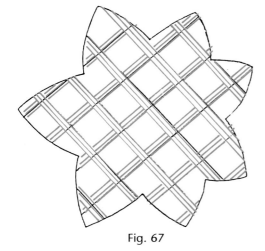

Fig. 67

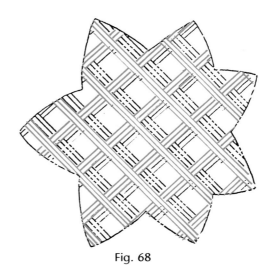

Fig. 68

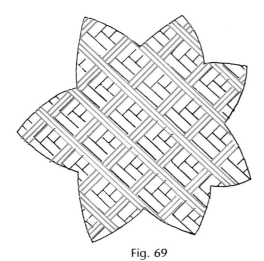

Fig. 69

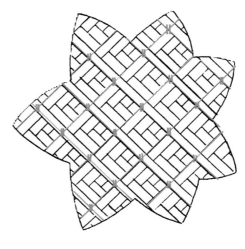

Fig. 70

■ THE STITCHES OF JAPANESE EMBROIDERY ■

Nw Novel: woven effect (mushiro-nui)

This technique conveys the impression of a woven surface. Using a thick thread (typically 4➜1) with a fairly tight twist, stitch two lines along the weft of the fabric, then leave the space of one thread open before stitching the next two lines. Cover the area of the figure in this way (Fig. 71). Be sure to maintain a consistent overtwist.

Next, stitch perpendicular lines of #1 gold, half hitch (see page 54), across this foundation at ¼ in intervals along the thread (Fig. 72). Keep the gold from twisting by using the stroking needle. To hold these gold threads in place, tie each one down at ⅜ in intervals across the thread (Fig. 73). Stitch (as always, from top to bottom) in the open spaces

between the foundation threads, and work from left to right, staggering the stitches from row to row.

Next fill the open spaces in the weft direction using the same thread as in the first stage (Fig. 74). Maintain a consistent overtwist. Tie down this last layer with gold-color silk thread (1➜1 twisted) or the color of the foundation, in the horizontal direction. Stitch these lines halfway between the previously stitched lines and use a back stitch motion (Figs 75–76).

Finally, to hide the stitching holes along the outer edge of the figure, a non-stitchable thread of the same color, along with a #4 gold or silver thread to frame it, should be laid along the edge and couched with 1➜2 twisted thread of the same color.

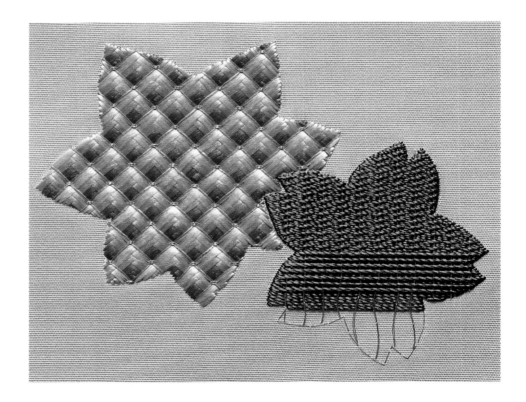

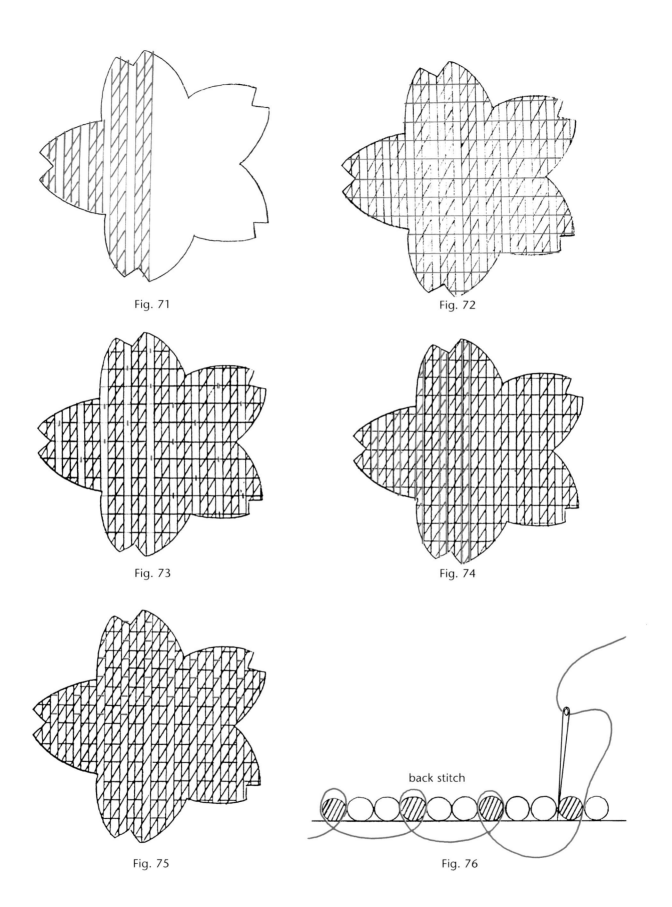

Fig. 71

Fig. 72

Fig. 73

Fig. 74

Fig. 75

back stitch

Fig. 76

Nb Novel: blister effect (hōkamuri-nui)

This simple technique adds three-dimensional variety to an otherwise uniform area. Make a knot (see pages 110-111) with a thick, twisted thread, then cover it completely with a long stitch of flat thread (Fig. 77).

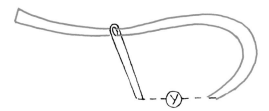

Fig. 77

PADDING

Various methods of padding are used to enhance the reflective quality of the silk, either flat or twisted. Cotton or silk padding threads may be stitched, or laid and couched, depending on the effect desired. Padding is also sometimes worked over card when a heavy, raised area is required and the threads to be supported are difficult to control. In addition, padding may be used simply to assist the stitcher in maintaining a regular shape (as in the *shippo* pattern). Padding techniques are used to lift up the embroidery and add contour and shading.

P_S Padding: stitched (hira-nikuire)

In all stitched padding, begin with a knot and tail which are left on the surface of the fabric. After a few stitches, pull up on the tail and cut off the knot. Padding is worked underneath (before) and at the opposite angle to the finished layer. Stitch one point (one needle hole) in from the outer line of the figure, and use the stroking needle to keep the laid stitch (not satin stitched) thread flat. Choose thread of the right thickness to achieve the desired height (thickness of padding), but taper off towards the inner, shaded portions of the figure. Tapering is done by using thinner thread, spacing the stitches, or mixing long and short stitches. Do not leave any knots on the underside of the fabric.

P_SV Padding: stitched, vertical direction

To pad a vertical layer, make stitches of cotton padding thread across the horizontal direction of the figure.

P_SH Padding: stitched, horizontal direction

To pad a horizontal layer, make stitches of cotton padding thread across the vertical direction of the figure (Fig. 78).

Below: PsH

Above right: PsD

P_SD Padding: stitched, diagonal direction (naname-nikuire)

To pad a diagonal layer, stitch the padding in the opposite diagonal from the final layer. Padding can be tapered to give a naturalistic effect (Fig. 79).

Fig. 78

Fig. 79

Pc Padding: couched (koma-nikuire)

Half hitch (see page 54) cotton threads on a *koma* (see page 42) and overtwist them into one thread of the desired thickness (no undertwisting is done). To pad the edges of a figure, lay the single line of twisted padding thread along the outer line of the figure and couch it carefully with white couching thread. Taper both ends about ¼–⅝ in and simply snip off the ends beyond the first and last couching (the ends are not pulled through the fabric). The embroidery of the figure is then stitched over this line of padding (Fig. 80).

This padding technique can also be used to raise the center of a figure, such as Braided: double central (see page 117). In this case, the couching can be less precise.

Fig. 80

FUZZY EFFECTS

Considered the technique of highest dignity in
Japanese embroidery, fuzzy effect is worked by laying
parallel stitches that do not touch and then by
holding them in various ways. This allows the
background fabric to show through and creates an
extremely subtle effect.

Fw Fuzzy: weft valley layer (sugabiki)

By leaving unfilled lines across the whole weft of the figure, this technique gives a very subdued, even fuzzy, effect. Thin (1➔1 twisted thread) lines are laid along the weft lines of a fabric with a well-defined weave (such as silk crepe), either in each valley of the weave (Fig. 81) or in every second valley (Fig. 82). The softness or tightness of the twist is determined by the overall effect desired.

If vertical holding (see page 108) is to be used, the thread should be twisted rather on the tight side and should be given added overtwist while the lines are being sewn. With diagonal holding (see page 109), a soft twist should be used and almost no overtwisting is needed while stitching.

To convey shadow and three-dimensions, the lines in the shaded areas are reduced to half-thickness. Take the 1➔1 twisted thread through the fabric and, overlapping the stitches just a tiny amount, continue the line with 1➔2 twisted thread for tapering.

Fig. 81

Fig. 82

Fv Fuzzy: vertically held valley lines (suganui-tojiosae)

One way to hold down the weft valley layer is with vertical stitches. Use thin 1➜2 twisted thread of the same color. Bring the needle up on the right side of the foundation thread, but within the same valley of weave (Fig. 83), and go down on the left side, still in the same valley. Work your way towards yourself down the whole length of this one valley. Then, passing the thread back under the fabric to the far side of the next valley, work down the next line, this time stitching half way between the stitches of the preceding line ('bricking'), and so on, staggering the stitches line by line, across the figure from left to right (Fig. 84).

Note that, although this technique is called vertically held valley lines, the stitches appear to be horizontal in the diagram, as it is oriented in the same direction as the work is when being stitched on the frame.

You can add a striking effect by placing gold or silver lines (or a half-strand of white flat silk) alongside the foundation lines. These lines, which must all be on the same side of the foundation lines, are stitched in the same valley with each foundation line and are held down at the same time as the foundation line. They are shorter than the original weft valley lines, and random in length. An extra couching stitch is taken wherever the 'striking effect' thread ends, even if it is in addition to the ordinary holding stitches. This technique is used only with vertical holding.

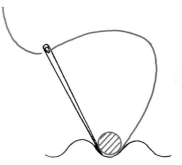

Fig. 83

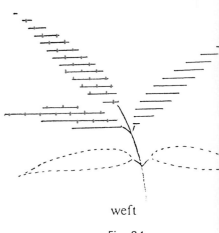

weft

Fig. 84

Fd Fuzzy: diagonally held valley lines (suganui-mojiriosae)

This holding technique gives an even fuzzier effect than vertically held valley lines. Using 1→2 twisted thread of the same color as the foundation layer, bring the needle up on the right side of the foundation thread and make a right diagonal stitch ¼ in or ⅜ in long, then go down on the left side. Be sure to stay within the same valley of weave. This time, however, instead of working all the way down one line at a time, work across the figure from left to right, then bring the needle back from below to the left side for the next row of stitches (Fig. 85).

The second row of holding interlocks with the first, beginning half-way along the length of the first row of stitches and going the same length beyond, and so on for every row following.

You can also change the effect by working some of these diagonal stitches in a different color. Do these first, then fill in the other stitches.

You may combine vertical and diagonal holding in the same figure. The diagonal stitches have a more pronounced effect than the vertical.

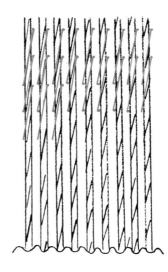

Fig. 85

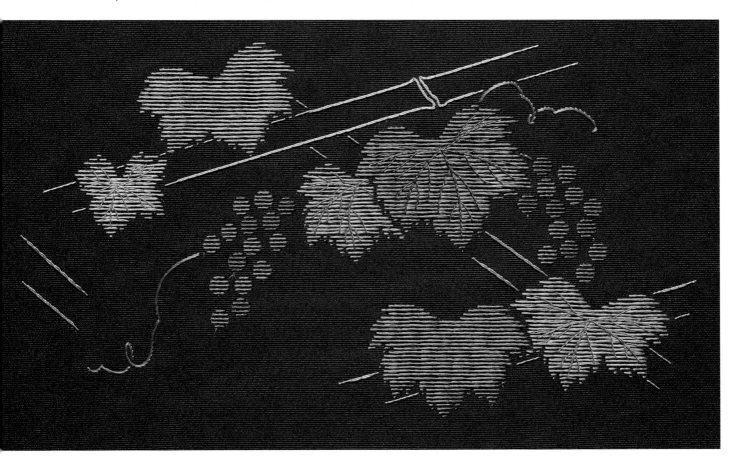

KNOTS

Knots, which were one of the earliest techniques used in embroidery in Japan, give texture to an otherwise flat work. They may be used individually to indicate random pieces of pollen, or massed in the center of a flower. Knots may vary in size and shape, for they can be used round and with tails.

Kr Knots: round (sagara-nui)

Using an S-twist thread, bring the needle up through the fabric. Loop the thread in the counter-clockwise direction. Pass the needle under the right side of the loop, over the left side of the loop, and into the fabric, slightly beyond the beginning point. Pull the needle through. You now have two loops above the fabric. Put two fingers of your right hand through

the near loop and spread it to pull the crossing point to the surface of the fabric. Then, as you pull the thread down through the fabric, a round knot is formed (Fig. 86).

Putting the stroking needle through the loop as you pull the thread makes it easier to position the knot.

This technique is used to fill areas or lines with knots. Make every knot in the same way with the same direction, right to left, top to bottom, or toward the center, staggering the knots row by row. When filling an area, contour and shading can be added, especially toward the inner parts of the figure, by using thinner thread, by spacing knots, or by changing the color (Fig. 87).

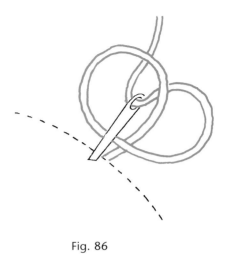

Fig. 86

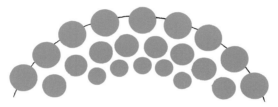

Fig. 87

KI Knots: long leg (ashinaga-sagara)

This is a round knot with a tail. Proceed as described in the instructions for single knots, except that the needle re-enters the fabric at a point away from the starting hole, the distance depending on how long a tail is desired. As the thread is pulled through the fabric, use the stroking needle to keep the loop over the starting hole, so that the knot is formed there (Fig. 88).

KI + Ra Knots: long leg + Realistic: alternating long and short

Long-legged knots can be combined with realistic, alternating long and short technique. Make radiating lines on your pattern to serve as guidelines. First, lay rather loosely pulled knots along the outer line of the figure; they should have rather long tails laid along the radiating lines of the pattern. The second row of knots is laid between the tails of the first row, and so on, row by row. The knots of the third row may be formed on top of the tails of the first row, and so on for later rows (Fig. 89).

Contour and shading may be added as desired, by using thinner thread, by spacing the knots, or by changing the color.

Above right: KI
Below: KI + Ra

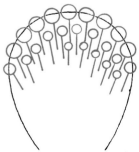

Fig. 88

Fig. 89

BRAIDED CORDS

Cords are used both as a design motif and as a design device. The various techniques employed are imitations of different *kumihimo* (Japanese braids). When used with antique mirrors, for example, cords represent handles, as they would actually have been used. Additional cords in the background, however, are simply a way of giving motion to the design.

Bw Braided: wicker (ajirokumi-nui)

Work in the direction in which the chevron points, whether towards or away from you. Stitch four adjoining diagonal lines which cross over the center of the figure. The ends of these lines will be covered over by the four diagonals coming next from the opposite direction. Use gradation of color for shading (Fig. 90).

Imitation-wicker braid

This technique is used for embroidering a cord with an imitation-wicker braid design, giving a chevron effect. While not a true braid, this stitch pattern gives a wicker effect by adding stitches on top of a diagonal single layer.

Use #1 metal thread, half hitched. (See page 54 for instructions on how to embroider with stitchable metal thread.) The stitches alternate between left diagonal (top left to bottom right) and right diagonal (top right to bottom left). The left diagonal stitch is longer than the right. The thread of each stitch hides the needle hole of the preceding stitch (Fig. 91).

Rein effect

To create a cord with a rein effect, start by couching pairs of metal threads to and fro (C$_2$t) along the cord until the width is filled. Using twisted silk thread, work a diagonal group of stitches across the metal threads, leaving a gap between bands of stitches which is equal to their width (Fig. 92).

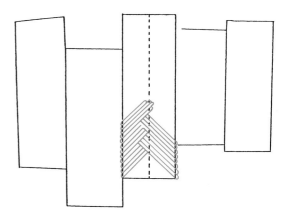

Fig. 90

Fig. 91

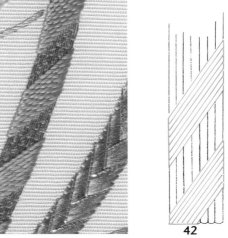

3
1

42

Fig. 92

Bs Braided: single central (nakayuwae-nui)

This technique results in a pattern of woven diamonds along the central line of the cord. While working long diagonal stitches, tie down every four long stitches with four short stitches along the opposite diagonal in such a way as to make a line of diamond-shaped figures along the central line of the cord. Be sure to give the thread a good overtwist while stitching (Fig. 93).

On very wide cords, two groups of four stitches may be used to tie down the long diagonal stitches, forming a double pattern of woven diamonds, 2Bs.

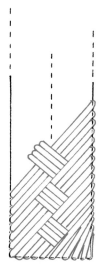

Fig. 93

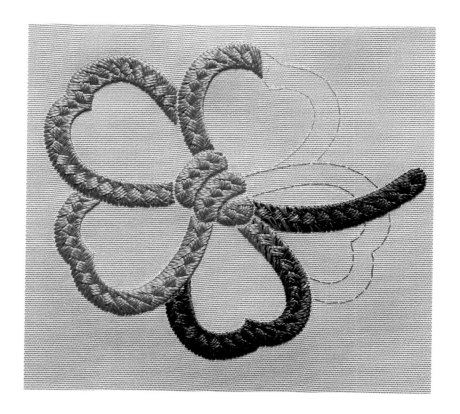

Bd Braided: double central (yotsugumi-nui)

This technique results in a three-dimensional cord with a double line of weave along the central line of the figure. Use a single thread of #4 gold to outline the figure, couching it at every twist with gold-color couching thread. Instead of cutting the ends of the gold thread at the ends of the figure, bend them back within the area of the figure, about ¼ in from the end, and couch them and cut them there (the so-called M-ending). Do not pull the ends through to the back. Lay a line of cotton padding twenty-four threads thick (or the thickness desired in the individual embroidery) down the center of the figure and couch it with white couching thread, tapering the ends to one-half thickness (Fig. 94).

Using either twisted or flat silk or #1 metallic thread, bring the needle up outside the outer edge of the gold thread and make four stitches each of alternating right and left diagonals. The diagonal stitches move towards you as usual, from top to bottom, but the working order is away from you

towards the opposite side of the figure. Each set of four stitches overlaps the preceding set of four to form a double row of diamond-shaped figures along the central line of the cord (Fig. 95). As a checkpoint, the second stitch of each group of four should be opposite the last stitch of the previous group. Be careful to maintain ninety degree intersections all the way, as well as a consistent overtwist in the thread. When blending threads, use a separate needle for each thread.

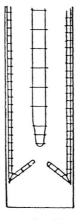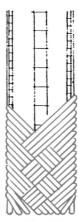

Fig. 94   Fig. 95

REALISTIC EFFECTS

Motifs from the realm of nature have always provided inspiration for Japanese embroidery designs, but in older works they are stylized and arranged. Shading is seldom used, and an entire flower would be stitched in one color. Nowadays realistic effects are employed to incorporate color changes within a motif in a manner that may be either stylized or casual. In order to achieve the most natural look, technique Rr (Realistic: random long and short) is used. For a stylized effect, technique Ra (Realistic: alternating long and short) gives a more formal look.

Before beginning the embroidery, draw the natural contour lines of the figure. For a flower like the pansy, this means determining the tips and sides of each figure (shape) which it contains.

For each figure, draw a central line dividing the figure in half, then divide each half in half. Again divide each area into half, so that you have the figure divided into eight areas. Finally divide the two side areas in half one more time. The edge of the motif outside these two lines is considered the outer edge.

The stitch direction, as always, is top to bottom or right to left. The working order on the figure is from the outer edge inwards, resulting in some stitches being taken in the opposite direction to others. The working order for each row is from the center of the figure to the right, then from center to left.

As the work progresses inwards toward the center row by row, you can use thinner thread and color gradation. The stitches either overlap or interlock.

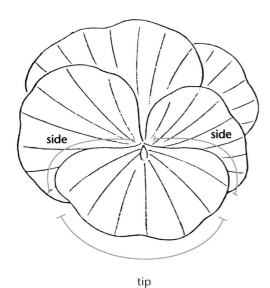

tip

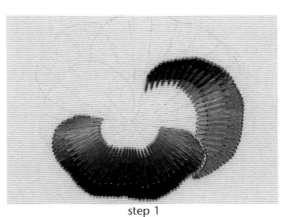

step 1

step 2

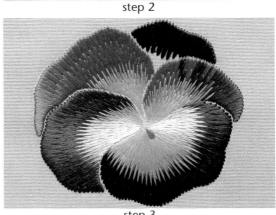

step 3

Ra Realistic: alternating long and short stitches (nagamijika-sashinui)

This technique fills up the area with alternating long and short stitches. Light-and-dark shading traverses the width of the figure.

For the first row, the natural flow of the lines radiating out from the center indicates the direction of the stitching. The first row is a line of alternating long and short stitches along the outer tip of the figure. The short stitches are about two-thirds the length of the longer ones (Fig. 96).

For the second row, use thinner thread. Bring the needle up or down at the mid-point of the shorter stitches of the first row. Pierce the thread. The stitches of the second row should extend beyond (and be the same length as) the longer stitches of the first row (Fig. 97).

For the third row, again, use thinner thread than that of the previous row. Bring the needle up (or down) at mid-point of the longer stitches of the first row (always piercing the thread). The stitches of the third row extend beyond those of the second row (Fig. 98).

Continue in the same way for other rows. As the lines converge toward the center, some stitches will simply be omitted. Attempt to have the stitches lined up neatly in lines radiating from the center of the design.

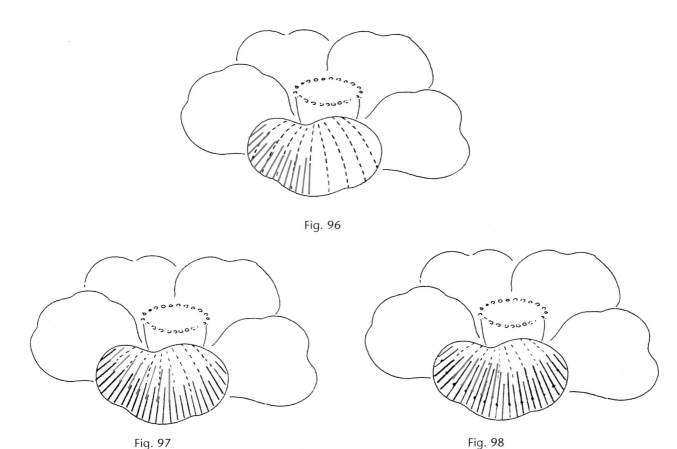

Fig. 96

Fig. 97

Fig. 98

Rr Realistic: random long and short stitches (midare-sashinui)

This technique uses long and short stitches at random. Light-and-dark shading is worked along the contour lines of the figure. In the first row, mix up long and short stitches in no exact order. The direction of the stitching is determined, of course, by the natural flow of the lines radiating out from the center of the design (Fig. 99).

For later rows, bring the needle up or down between the stitches of the preceding rows (not through the thread). Rather than do a full row across, work area by area and concentrate on shading (Fig. 100). The stitches are not uniform in length and the rows are not clear. It is not necessary to change the thickness of the thread as often as in alternating long and short stitches.

Fig. 99   Fig. 100

Rc Realistic: curved angular stitches (kussetsu-sashinui)

This technique is used for showing shading on larger petals of one solid color.

Use only flat silk and one color. There is no need to draw radiating lines of the pattern. Draw a few lines down the length of the figure. The natural contour is conveyed with angular bends along the length of these lines.

Work from the center to the right, then to the left. The first row will have longer and shorter stitches according to the line of the outer tip of the figure (Fig. 101). Stitch parallel, not radiating, stitches in each row. Do not align the up and down needle holes too neatly; let there be a certain irregularity. Use overlapping stitches at the angular joints, coming up between the threads a point in from the end of the previous stitch (Fig. 102). Hardly any variation is needed in the thickness of the thread.

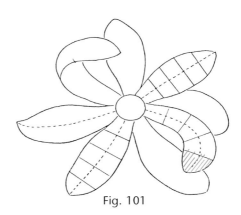

Fig. 101

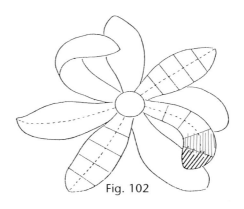

Fig. 102

GLOSSARY

anesama doll made of folded, colored paper

bugaku ancient dance of the court nobles

buri-buri barrel-shaped object with wheels on one end used as a child's toy

choken light-weight dancing cloak

Chugu-ji Buddhist nunnery in Nara where the oldest extant Japanese embroidery is kept

daimyo feudal lord, occupying the highest position in the warrior class except for the *shōgun*

eras (*nengō*)

    Asuka (552–645)

    Nara (645–794)

    Heian (794–1185)

    Kamakura (1185–1392)

    Muromachi (1392–1568)

    Momoyama (1568–1615)

    Edo (1615–1868)

    Meiji (1868–1912)

    Taisho (1912–1926)

    Showa (1926–1989)

    Heisei (1989–)

gagaku ancient ceremonial music of the court nobles

geisha female entertainers, who master the arts of music, dance and conversation so that they might provide companionship to their patrons or customers

gekokujō term used to describe a situation when persons of lower status replace their former superiors in the political hierarchy

han-eri silken scarf, sometimes embroidered, which is worn inside the neck of a *kimono*

haniwa baked clay sculptures used to decorate 4–7th century tombs

haori traditional jacket worn over a *kimono*

hippari-toji line of held thread technique

happi straight, short-sleeved coat usually made of cotton or linen

Hōryū-ji 'treasure house' in Nara Prefecture which is renowned for its spectacular collection of ancient Japanese art works

iro-iri karaori costume which features red in the background color, making it suitable for a young female costume

iro-nashi karaori costume without red, designed to be worn by an actor playing the role of an older woman

jūni-hitoe the twelve-layered formal court ensemble worn by ladies-in-waiting of the Heian Period

kabuki form of Japanese theater, using dance and music as well as acting

kaeshi-nui back stitch

kana general term used for the system of writing the sounds of Japanese words, rather than characters which represent the meaning of words

kara-ori twill weave fabric used for *Nō* costume, where long floats of thread create patterns which resemble embroidery

kari-ginu originally a garment for hunting, later adopted by *Nō* actors

kasane no irome layered color tones

kawari-nui novel effect

kazuke-mono literally, reward clothing. (Refers to clothing given by nobility to *Nō* drama actors to reward their talent.)

kimono traditional garment, tied with a sash (*obi*), worn in Japan by both men and women

koshimaki form of *kosode* decorated with small, repeating patterns. In the Muromachi period, this type of *kosode* was worn over the outer *kosode*, tied at the waist with a supporting *obi*, and allowed to drape from the waistline of the wearer.

kosode small-sleeved garment which preceded the *kimono*

koto thirteen-stringed wooden instrument which is plucked like a zither

kuni state

kura traditional Japanese storehouse, or treasure house

kusari-nui chain stitch

mandala work of art used for meditation and ritual in which religious doctrine is portrayed by means of symbols (The Japanese word *mandara* is the Japanese transliteration of the Japanese pronunciation of the Chinese characters.)

matsui-nui outline stitch

mizu-goromo unlined traveling cloak

nari-jibiki horizontal foundation layer

nengō era names (Japan is the only country in the world still using this method of reckoning time by the year of the Emperor's reign. Upon the death of the emperor Showa in January, 1989, the name Heisei was adopted for the new era, so that events for that year are said to have happened in Heisei 1.)

nioi fragrance

Nō the oldest type of theater in Japan, highly ritualized

nui-eri embroidered scarf *(han-eri)* worn with *kimono*

nui-haku decoration of fabric with embroidery and gold leaf

nuikiri diagonal single layer

nuki-jibiki weft foundation layer

obi sash tied around the waist of a *kimono*

obi-jime decorative cord tied on top of the *obi* to hold it in place

ōsode long-sleeved garment worn by Heian aristocracy

renga form of highly structured poetry which flourished from the thirteenth to the sixteenth centuries

sagara-nui knot stitch

sarugaku a form of entertainment which predated *Nō*, initially involving acrobats and jugglers, which evolved into a form of drama

sashi-nui realistic effect

seikaiha traditional Japanese decorative pattern of overlapping half-circles which has come to symbolize ocean waves

shibori resist dyeing technique in which the fabric is folded, gathered with thread, or sheathed to prevent the dye from reaching selected areas (refers to the dye technique and the fabric produced)

shibori-eri tie-dyed scarf *(han-eri)* worn with *kimono*

shippo pattern of overlapping circles or ovals which is used to symbolize expansiveness

shishū embroidery

shō wind instrument with a cup-shaped body from which seventeen bamboo pipes protrude. Sound is produced by either sucking or blowing into the mouth hole.

shō-chiku-bai the use of pine, plum, and bamboo together in the same design as a symbol for happiness. This motif is also called the 'three friends of winter'.

shōgun top military ruler

sobatsugi sleeveless coat worn by *Nō* actors when playing a Chinese character

suikan brocade fabric stiffened with starch and lacquer

suo garment made of stencil-dyed, inexpensive fabric, worn by actors in *Nō* drama when playing a male peasant

suri-haku technique whereby metal leaf is rubbed or pressed into an area of adhesive applied by means of a stencil

sutra scrolls scrolls containing Buddhist religious texts

taiko bashi a bridge which, seen in profile, has the rounded shape of a traditional Japanese drum (*taiko*)

taiko-musubi drum-style *obi*, most generally used in Japan today

takarazukushi group of motifs known as 'traditional treasures'. These include the magic sedge hat, straw rain cape, mallet, pearl or ball, balance scale, etc. Each represents a wish for health or good fortune.

Tokugawa shōgunate hereditary military dictatorship (1603–1868)

tomesode long-sleeved garment

torikabuto brocade helmet worn by court dancers

tsugibari-nui double running stitch

usuyo white appearance

yushiki 'having knowledge', taking part in the rites of the imperial court

yūshikisha those participating in the court rituals

yūsoku people with professional rank

yuzen-eri scarf *(han-eri)* decorated with paste-resist dyeing techniques worn with *kimono*

yuzen-zome paste-resist dyeing

yūshoku pertaining to ancient customs and ceremonies of the Japanese court

BIBLIOGRAPHY

Brandon, Rieko. 'Feminine Elegance: Japanese Kimonos from the Academy's Textile Collection', *Calendar News*, Honolulu, Honolulu Academy of Arts, March/April, 1996, pp. 4-5

Dalby, Liza Crihfield. *Kimono*, New Haven, CT, Yale University Press, 1993

Gluckman, Dale Carolyn, and Sharon Sadako Takeda. *When Art Became Fashion: Kosode in Edo-Period Japan*, Los Angeles, CA, Los Angeles County Museum of Art, 1992

Hays, Ralph V. and Mary E. *The Shojiro Nomura Fukusa Collection*, Oakland, CA, The Mills College Art Gallery, 1983

Ishimura, Hayao and Nobuhiko Maruyama, and Tomoyuki Yamanobe. *Robes of Elegance: Japanese Kimonos of the 16th–20th Centuries*, tr Haruko Ward, Raleigh, NC, Carolina Museum of Art, 1988

Ito, Toshiko. *Tsujigahana: The Flower of Japanese Textile Art*, tr Monica Bethe, New York, Kodansha, 1981

Joly, Henri L. *Legend in Japanese Art*, Rutland VT, Charles E. Tuttle, 1967 (originally published London, John Lane, The Bodley Head, 1908)

Kennedy, Alan. *Japanese Costume: History and Tradition*, Paris, Editions Adam Biro, 1990

Kodansha Encyclopedia of Japan, Tokyo, Kodansha, 1983

Kyoto Shoin's Art Library of Japanese Textiles (vols 1–11), Kyoto Shoin, 1993: 1. *Shōsō in Textiles*, 2. *Tsujigahana*, 3. *Clothes of Samurai Warriors*, 4. *Kosode Kimono*, 5. *Yūzen Dyeing*, 6. *Furisode Kimono*, 7. *Japanese Embroidery*, 8. *Noh Costumes*, 9. *Kyōgen Costumes*, 10. *Kabuki Costumes*, 11. *Japanese Tie-dyeing*

Kurenai: Japanese Embroidery Journal, Roswell, GA, Embroidery Research Press, 1988 to present

Liddell, Jill. *The Story of the Kimono*, New York, E.P. Dutton, 1989

Minnich, Helen Benton. *Japanese Costume and the Makers of Its Elegant Tradition*, Rutland, VT, Charles E. Tuttle, 1963

Mizoguchi, Saburo. *Design Motifs*, Arts of Japan Series (1), New York, Weatherhill/Shibundo, 1973

Nagasaki, Iwao, and Monica Bethe. *Patterns and Poetry: Noh Robes in the Lucy Truman Aldrich Collection at the Museum of Art, Rhode Island School of Design*, Providence, RI, Rhode Island School of Design, 1992

Nishimura, Hyobu, Jean Mailey, and Joseph S. Hayes, Jr. *Tagasode: Whose Sleeves? Kimono from the Kanebo Collection*, New York, Japan Society, 1976

Niwa, Motoji. *Japanese Traditional Patterns (1): Plants, Animals, Phenomena*, Tokyo, Graphc-sha Publishing Co., 1990
Japanese Traditional Patterns (2): Structure and Implements, Geometric Patterns, Family Crests, Tokyo, Graphc-sha Publishing Co., 1990

Yamanobe, Tomoyuki, and Kenzo Fukii. *Kyoto Modern Textiles: 1868–1940*, Kyoto, Kyoto Textile Wholesalers Association, 1996

USEFUL ADDRESSES

JAPANESE EMBROIDERY CENTERS WORLDWIDE

Margaret Lewis
White Lodge
Littlewick Road
Lower Knaphill
Woking, Surrey
GU21 2JU
U K
Phone: (01483) 476246
Fax: (01483) 836152

Maureen Moore
32 Brook Street
Lower Hutt, 6009
New Zealand
Phone: 64-4-5696-692
Fax: 64-4-5696-692

Dianne Nicholson
1378 Nelson Place
Kelowna, BC V1Y 9H4
Canada
Phone: (250) 862-5818
Fax: (250) 862-8297

Lesley Sullivan-Bourne
P.O. Box 855
Morphett Vale, SA 5162
Australia
Phone: 61-8-8325-3434
Fax: 61-8-8325-3434

Japanese Embroidery Center
2727 Spalding Drive
Dunwoody,
GA 30350-4623
USA
Phone: (770) 390-0617
Fax: (770) 512-7837

INDEX OF TECHNIQUES